Changing Organizations from Within

Changing Organizations from Within

Roles, Risks and Consultancy Relationships

SUSAN ROSINA WHITTLE
and

ROBIN C. STEVENS

Routledge
Taylor & Francis Group

LONDON AND NEW YORK

First published in paperback 2024

First published 2013 by Gower Publishing

Published 2016 by Routledge
4 Park Square, Milton Park, Abingdon, Oxon OX14 4RN

and by Routledge
605 Third Avenue, New York, NY 10158

Routledge is an imprint of the Taylor & Francis Group, an informa business

British Library Cataloguing in Publication Data
Changing organizations from within : roles, risks and
    consultancy relationships.
    1. Organizational change--Management. 2. Business
    consultants.
    I. Whittle, Sue. II. Stevens, Robin C.
    658.4'6-dc23

Library of Congress Cataloging-in-Publication Data
Changing organizations from within : roles, risks and consultancy
relationships / [edited] by Susan Rosina Whittle and Robin C. Stevens.
    p. cm.
    Includes bibliographical references and index.
    ISBN 978-1-4094-4968-3 (hbk) -- ISBN 978-1-4094-4969-0 (ebk)
    -- ISBN 978-1-4094-7472-2 (epub) 1. Organizational change--Case
    studies. 2. Consultants--Case studies. I. Whittle, Sue. II. Stevens, Robin
    C.
    HD58.8.C4628 2013
    658.4'06--dc23

                                                                          2012040291

    ISBN: 978-1-4094-4968-3 (hbk)
    ISBN: 978-1-03-283736-9 (pbk)
    ISBN: 978-1-315-57126-3 (ebk)

    DOI: 10.4324/9781315571263

Contents

List of Figures

List of Tables

About the Editors

Dr Susan Rosina Whittle BA, MSc, PhD, MIC

I combine my work as an independent consultant with my professional development role as Director of The Tavistock Institute Practitioner Certificate in Consulting and Change. In my consultancy work, I specialize in helping clients to introduce new ways of thinking and working to address organizational needs and problems. I have consulted to directors, managers, change agents, consultants, teams, and groups in many sectors, including manufacturing, government, health, construction, philanthropy, and the prison service. Typical assignments include: consortium building in contexts of resource scarcity; loss of trust in multi-organizational initiatives; responding to externally driven culture change; and consulting to strategy options in contested contexts. Much of my work now is with internal and external organization development and change consultants, helping them to craft an authoritative presence by enhancing their repertories and sustaining their identities in tough working environments.

I have published in academic and practitioner journals and co-edited *Mind-ful Consulting* (2009, London: Karnac Books). I have taught programs in Organization Development, Quality Management, and Research Methods at Masters level in a number of universities and served as external examiner at Manchester and Brighton Business Schools. From 2001 to 2009 I held a core faculty role on The Tavistock Institute's Advanced Organizational Consultation Masters programme and until 2011 held a core faculty role on Birmingham University's MA in Leading Public Service Change and Organizational Development. I can be contacted at sue@whittle1.karoo.co.uk

Robin C. Stevens JD, MA

I am an organizational consultant who also has extensive experience in the management of complex functions. I consult to large public agencies and other organizations that want to improve their effectiveness in the areas of procurement, supply chain management, and project management, most often to improve their ability to deliver large capital programs and projects or maintenance operations. My work involves helping them improve their organizational design and processes and procedures. I work with diverse groups of professionals to establish the policies, procedures, and working relationships necessary to improve these functions and operations.

My interest and expertise in these areas arose through my work at New York City Transit, which operates the subways and buses in New York City. I began work there as a lawyer with a specialty in contract negotiation and then went on to manage procurement and supply chain functions. I served as the Vice President, Materiel Division, which is responsible for the agency's procurement, contract administration, and inventory management functions. I hold a Master of Arts in Advanced Organizational Consultation from the City University London in conjunction with The Tavistock Institute. I served as the Director and for over ten years was on the faculty of the Organization Program of the William Alanson White Institute in New York City. The program offered mid-career professionals the chance to learn about organizational dynamics to improve their effectiveness at work.

For the last three years I have worked with colleagues to deliver workshops about the application of psychoanalytic theories to group and organizational life for psychologists and other social service professionals at Kyoto Bunkyo University.

I can be contacted at robin@robinstevensconsulting.com

About the Contributors

Lord Victor O. Adebowale, MA, CBE

Victor is the CEO of Turning Point, a national provider of social care services, and has over 25 years experience of leading not for profit services in housing, homelessness, criminal justice, substance misuse and employment services. He has taken leadership positions in developing public policy on employment and health. He writes regularly for *Housing Today, Community Care* and other specialist and mainstream publications. Victor is Director of Leadership in Mind OD Consultancy and a board member of St Vincent's health IT consulting. In 2000, he was awarded the CBE and in 2001 became a Crossbench member of the House of Lords.

Andrew Day BSc (Hons), MSc, C.Psychol, D. Psych, D.C. Psych

Andrew works as an Organization Development Consultant at Ashridge Consulting, part of Ashridge Business School in the UK. He specializes in helping individuals, groups and organizations to develop, change and work through transitions. He seeks to support collaboration and participation in the process of change in organizations. He is informed by systems psychodynamic theory, gestalt and social psychology and complexity theory. Prior to joining Ashridge, he worked as an internal Organization Development consultant in a global automotive manufacturer. Andrew is a Chartered Occupational Psychologist with Doctorates in Occupational Psychology and Counselling Psychology and Psychotherapy. He is an alumni of the Tavistock Institute's AOC programme.

Lisa Gardiner BHSc, M.AppSc (Org Dev)

Lisa provides consultancy to organizations in human services, including government and non-government organizations throughout Australia. Her key areas of consultancy include developing models of service in collaboration with the organization and creating unique learning experiences for individuals and groups. She utilizes current research in neuroscience, linking that to improved outcomes in leadership and personal/professional development in the workplace. She has over 25 years experience working in direct service provision, organizational development, training and management.

Pauline Holland MA, MPhil

Pauline (Pauline@taylorclarke.co.uk) is a Principal Consultant with Taylor Clarke, a full service organizational effectiveness and development consultancy based in Scotland, UK. She works with organizations to optimize individual, group and organizational performance by developing the system's capacity for sense-making, learning and change. She brings a deep understanding of group and organizational dynamics to her work with clients, helping them to access and utilize deeper, often hidden sources of knowing that foster innovation and creativity. Pauline is an interim board member and conference planning group member of the newly established ODNEurope, the European Chapter of the Organisational Development Network, an international professional association of organizational development practitioners.

Karen Izod MA, CQSW

Karen works in the field of organizational change and professional development from her consultancy practice KIzod Consulting. This provides a platform for collaborative enterprise with client systems, and fellow consultants and academics. She is a Director of the Tavistock Institute's Practitioner Certificate in Consulting and Change, and former Co-Director of their Coaching for Leadership and Professional Development programme. She works extensively with experiential approaches, helping clients generate models and conditions for change which emphasize professional presence and agility in role. Her early career was in social work: as a practitioner, in public sector management and internal consultancy.

Gerhard Raftl BA Psych, MA Psych

Gerhard is a Director at SAL Consulting and Principal Psychologist. He has been a Clinical Psychologist and practitioner for more than 25 years. He was previously the manager of a State-wide Behaviour Intervention Service. His experience includes the review of organizational approaches, procedures, practice and risk management in human services environments. As a senior clinical supervisor, he provides direction and practice improvement across a number of government and non-government organizations.

Elizabeth Summers BA Psych

Elizabeth is a Director at SAL Consulting, a Human Services Consultant and Behaviour Support Specialist. She has more than 12 years experience delivering training, clinical support, systems, policy development and quality assurance and improvement services to government and non-government human service organizations. She is passionate about assisting people to implement theoretical frameworks into day-to-day practice.

Sally R. Wigutow MSc

Sally is an organizational consultant who has worked with family owned and managed enterprise for over 20 years. She consults to first generation founders and next generation leadership on issues of succession, management development and on the alignment between operations and governance. Her practice focuses on working in collaboration with clients to create organizational structures and processes that increase effectiveness in these arenas while at the same time identifying and making use of the powerful impact of family relationships.

Preface and Acknowledgements

This book came about at the instigation of my co-editor, Susan Rosina Whittle, who noticed the dearth of literature about, by, and for organizational consultants who practice from the inside in some way. We had many discussions about what constitutes an insider and came up with a somewhat expansive definition in terms of the number of titles one could hold and still be an insider, but at heart the defining characteristic is simple: consultants who feel themselves to be in some way part of the organizations they consult to. It's been a difficult, frustrating and rewarding journey from those conversations to this book. Our authors have become a group and we've enacted many of the dynamics that are part of group life. This has been a project, with all the frustrations that project life entails. We hope that at the end of this book you will have learned something new about group, professional and project life – something that will help you in your practice.

I want to thank Susan for having invited me into this project and helped me along the way. Her help has taken various forms: at times she refused to continue talking when I needed to be writing, she has pushed me to revise more when I hoped I was through, and we have engaged in intense debates about the role of an editor and what it means to be co-editors. We have lived the organizational dynamics that we write about. We hope that as you read this book, you will learn more about those dynamics and how they affect you, your clients, and your work with them.

We want to thank our contributors for making visible what many keep hidden and our publishers for their prompt and helpful advice and encouragement.

Robin C. Stevens and Susan Rosina Whittle

Introduction: Consultancy Roles, Risks and Relationships

Susan Rosina Whittle

What is This Book About?

This is an unusual book. It's about changing organizations from the inside. Many books on the practice of change are written by or for external consultants or by academics researching those with insider change roles, people such as organization development (OD) consultants, project leaders, or HR specialists (Wright 2009 and Sturdy et al. 2010). Yet many of us are expected to change our organizations from within, taking up roles to improve performance, develop capacity, change structures, manage crises, focus commitment, grow talent, or evaluate innovations. These roles have a range of titles, from specialist change roles, such as HR Business Partner, Learning and Development Manager and Team Facilitator, to roles that have organizational change at their heart but not necessarily in their titles. Examples include Project Manager, Trainer, Strategic Planner and CEO. This book is written by people with experience of working in these types of roles and draws on their work in manufacturing, social services, voluntary organizations, national and local government, construction and transport. It is written for insiders by insiders.

We also have contributions from external consultants. Why include externals in a book about change from within? Well, each of them writes about how sentience or belonging configures their client work. We use the Miller and Rice definition of a sentient system as 'one that demands loyalty from its members' (Miller and Rice 1967: 259). In Chapter 6, Sally R. Wigutow writes about 'Family Business: Inside and Outside the Systems at Play' and describes how she and her colleague became enmeshed unconsciously in the insider/

outsider dynamics of a family business. In Chapter 7, Lisa Gardiner, Elizabeth Summers and Gerhard Raftl explain how they position different types of consultants (clinical, leadership and organization development) inside their client organizations and analyze the consultant system to inform their interventions. That's why they can work 'By Invitation Only?'. Karen Izod, writing in Chapter 8, explores the challenge of maintaining boundaries in associate relationships that are 'Too Close for Comfort?'. Each of these chapters contributes to our understanding of the benefits and perils of insider-ness from a different perspective and offers strategies and techniques useful to those of us working to change organizations from within.

Through stories and case studies, the contributors to this book share practical advice, models and concepts to help insiders find their authority, make sense of tricky and unanticipated situations, and work more mindfully to help organizations change (Whittle 2009). Their chapters are not blue prints for 'how to do it' but accounts of what really happens when faced with change from within. The authors have different kinds of insider relationships with their organizations. Some are employees without an explicit 'change' label. Some feel themselves to be inside and yet call the organization for which they work their client. Some are external consultants or associates of consulting firms whose work depends on relating as an insider while retaining an external role and identity.

All our authors practice psycho-dynamically. This means they are consistently available, both relationally and emotionally, to their clients and strive to develop 'a capacity to remain consistently self-reflective and self-critical' (The Association for Psychodynamic Practice and Counseling in Organizational Settings). Practicing in this way means being able to articulate what makes us anxious and how anxiety can impact our competence. As we work in novel, risky or difficult situations, we develop routines and practices to contain our anxieties and emotions so that we can help our clients contain theirs and so risk changing. Appreciation of client fears and concerns and their ways of coping with them is gained by working with the client's transference. Transference is the unconscious transfer of feelings and behaviours from the past onto a person or situation in the present, for example, when my client behaves towards me as they would behave towards a parent, sibling, child or spouse. (See Robin Stevens, Chapter 9 in this book, for a fuller description.) There is a potential cost to working with the client's transference in that I can take on characteristics and issues that are projected onto me. Unwittingly, I can be changed from within by my client and find myself colluding with the client (perhaps relating to the client as a parent or sibling) rather than confronting the client's routines and behaviours (Heron 2001). If we are in touch with our thoughts and feelings, we have a capacity to use ourselves as instruments (Cheung-Judge 2001) to understand and to diagnose what *is* happening and what *needs* to happen to change our clients' organizations. Being aware of what my client stirs up in me is critical to this type of work.

What This Book Aims to Do

The premise of this book is that thinking explicitly as an insider can alert consultants and change agents to a number of relational issues and dynamics that otherwise can undermine competence and compromise practice (Izod 2008). These include: perpetual pulls on role and identity; lack of explicit contracting and evaluation; ever present narcissistic risks and the anxious defence of reputation; neglect of membership and boundary dynamics; and the influence of loyalty and family-like relationships on claims of success and allocation of blame. Our aim is to help readers recognize the power of these insider dynamics to shape organizational change by identifying the connections between consultants and change agents and their client organization (Bateson 1972). Choosing how to relate to clients and organizations in ways that support change requires us to be aware of what tugs at our identity and sense of worth; what evokes anxiety about our authority to act and take responsibility; and what mobilizes us to want to be near to some people and situations and flee others. This implies moving away from *both* a distanced, advisory or expert mode and from a more collegial and hands-on mode of leading change towards modes of practice that alert us to becoming too far in or staying too far out (Boggs and Rantisi 2003).

We expect this book to be of interest to change agents, internal consultants, leaders and managers who are engaged in changing organizations of which they are members. It will appeal to externals who are working with internals and want to understand the dynamics they encounter and to external consultants who are taking up internal change roles and want to better understand the challenges of changing organizations from within by using themselves as instruments. Academic and training institutions that provide professional development courses in organization consulting and change management, project management and other management development courses will find the cases and range of perspectives a valuable resource.

Insider Dynamics: Emerging Themes

Knowledge about changing organizations from within seems to be in a position not dissimilar to that of Organization Development some 40 or so years ago. While there is a vast and growing literature on concepts and methods, albeit largely written by externals and academics, the literature about the people doing the work is 'very meager' (Ganesh 1978: 1). Back then, Ganesh argued for more work to help us understand consultants and their styles because:

> *It is through an understanding of styles that one can begin to appreciate and understand the process of application of behavioral science knowledge to the development of organizations. (Ganesh 1978: 1)*

The contributors to this book share a conviction that understanding insider/ outsider dynamics is particularly useful to bringing about organizational change. While their stories and their styles differ, some themes appear in the writing. Among these are the dynamics of role giving and taking; power and political influence; identity and belonging; authority and expertise; risk, reputation and relationships.

Some of these are addressed explicitly by the authors. For example, Andrew Day takes us through some thinking about power before applying these ideas to his case. Lisa Gardiner and colleagues describe how consulting roles expanded and contracted unexpectedly over three phases of work with City-Care. Karen Izod writes about authority and identity when working as an associate and Sally R. Wigutow describes her encounters with risk when working with family businesses. As several authors refer to ways in which role taking, risks and relationships are powerful influences on their practice, I want to say a few words about 'style' by considering these three themes.

1   ROLE TAKING

Change agents are 'individuals whose primary role is to deliberately intervene into social systems in order to facilitate or bring about social change' (Tichy 1975: 772). This chimes with the theory-in-use in this book that, as change agents, consultants, leaders and managers are interventionists (Argyris 1970) and we would add *authorized by their organizations to intervene*. We are not concerned with those who try to subvert, overthrow or change their organizations secretly or by stealth. Such individuals are not agents of their organizations, although they may feel they are acting in the best interests of their organization. (See

Hoyle 2004 for an interesting paper on saboteurs and sycophants.) But being authorised to act (by job title, job description, resourcing, or request) still leaves significant choices about how to take up one's role (Krantz and Maltz 1997).

In her chapter, Pauline Holland describes how:

> ... *we never explicitly discussed my role. All the discussions we had about the change initiative were informal and took place within the context of the line manager-direct report relationship. This lack of explicit agreement about roles, not surprisingly, created some difficulties in our working relationship ... and I was left to try to make sense of what had happened between the Director and me and to consider what my experience might tell me about taking up an internal consulting role with one's manager as the primary client. (Holland 2013: 54, in this book)*

An early typology classifies change agent roles into catalyst, solution giver, process helper and resource linker:

- In a catalyst role, a change agent 'prods people' to get things started;

- In a solution giver role, agents offer clear ideas about what the change should be;

- Expertise on how to change is provided by the change agent taking a process role;

- The role of resource linker is taken up when people inside or outside the client system need to be brought together (Havelock 1973, Ottaway 1983).

A few more classifications are now available. Table I.1, on the following page, shows some of the better known schemes that have something to say about insider change roles.

Having access to a repertoire of roles can be a vital asset in organizational change, enabling practitioners to choose how they bring themselves to the work in ways that are best suited to the tasks in hand (Berg 2002). At the same time, not having the security and safety offered by a well defined and prescribed role can also be a source of uncertainty and anxiety, as Pauline Holland found 'I found it difficult to navigate skillfully the multiple roles that I occupied,

Table I.1   Some classifications of insider change roles

Classification Rationale	Roles	Source
Four consulting roles based on type of knowledge and inside/ outside boundary location.	Adviser, Provider, Partner, Implementer.	Kitay and Wright 2003
Four-fold structural typology of change agency	Change agents as Leaders, as Middle Managers, as Consultants, as Teams.	Caldwell 2003
Four (interventionist) roles of the HR practitioner.	Strategic partner, administrative expert, employee champion and change agent.	Ulrich 1997
Consulting Roles differentiated according to styles, professional expertise and types of tasks.	Expert, Pair of Hands, Process Consultant.	Schein 1988 Block 1981
Differences between the practice of external and internal OD consultants in planned change over the consulting life-cycle.	Roles of internal consultants are characterised by confusion, compartmentalisation, marginality, continuity, client expectations and departmental jealousy.	Lacey 1995

namely, my functional, organizational and professional roles' (Holland 2013: 55, in this book).

Wright refers to internal consultants as 'outsiders within' who 'need to act outside the hierarchy' and 'stress their objectivity and independence in advising clients and solving their problems'. If they succeed, internal consultants and change agents inhabit 'a highly ambiguous space' and much more so than external consultants (Wright 2009: 311). A colleague, in an internal consultant role with a large petro-chemical company, explained to me how he battled constantly with the invitation '… to get lost, by losing one's focus or perspective, or succumbing to subtle unconscious dynamics of resistance in the wider client system. As an internal consultant, one is invited to lose one's role in response to the internal pulls of the culture that resist change'.

The desire to belong, to be acknowledged as an insider, while needing to take an outsider stance in order to practice competently, is felt as a contradiction that requires on-going identity work (Wright 2009). We know there is more than one 'i' in identity. Failure to figure out 'who am I in this situation' makes role taking problematic.

Role taking means making the opportunity to select from the sorts of roles listed in Table I.1. Roles should be chosen that are appropriate to the work of organizational change for this client, at this time and in this place. My sense of *who I am in this situation* often governs the roles available to me. This sense of who I am can be influenced by:

1.   Hierarchy: if I experience myself in a reporting role to a manager or director, then the role of implementer may seem a more obvious choice than the role of expert or partner.

2.   Time: a felt need to act quickly or respond to my client immediately can easily push me into expert and provider roles and away from advisory and process consulting roles.

3.   Experience: if asked to do something that is 'Not Me', where a role is required outside my usual repertoire, then I may not know what to do or feel too out of my comfort zone to step into that role. We find this is a common scenario for internal consultants learning to consult to group process.

4.   Habit: as time passes, insiders can easily lose their distinctiveness and become 'part of the furniture'. For this reason, the life span of *an effective* internal consultant, able to balance and call on insider and outsider aspects of role and identity, may be limited (Wright 2009: 320, Caldwell 2003).

Being perceived as a reliable insider or an independent outsider may need to be negotiated constantly, with different client groups and subsystems, even if you are the CEO. In Chapter 3, Victor O. Adebowale relates how he established his role as CEO with the Board of Community Trust 'without any formal contracting process'. He goes on to describe how he worked with unspoken strategic debates in the organization 'to negotiate consulting interventions with the board of CT, the executive and senior managers and the frontline workers within the business' (Adebowale: 68, in this book). It is only much later that Victor realizes he had role taking choices and conceptualizes the role taken as that of an internal consultant working at the boundary on organizational identity. Victor's experiences suggest that opportunities to take roles as 'outsiders within' may be more readily available on entry and in the early days of working with a client. I would agree that there is greater need for vigilance the longer I work with my clients. I think about myself along an imaginary insider-outsider continuum. I find a ready-reckoner of the sort depicted in Figure I.1 a useful tool for the analysis of how insider/outsider

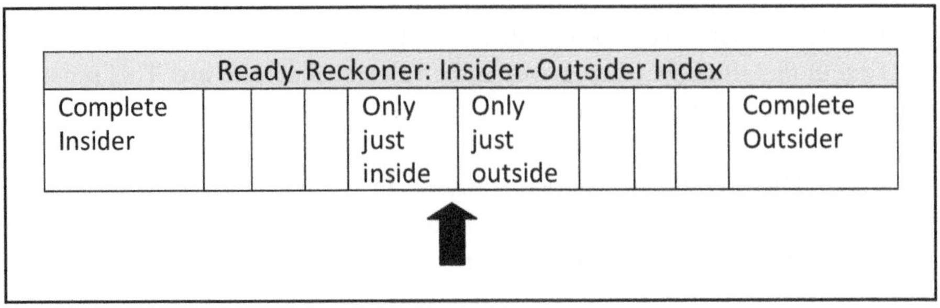

Ready-Reckoner: Insider-Outsider Index							
Complete Insider			Only just inside	Only just outside			Complete Outsider

Figure I.1   Insider-outsider ready-reckoner

I am perceived across different groups in a client system and how insider/ outsider I feel over time.

What do I notice to help me plot my location on the Index? Table I.2 shows some of the things that catch my attention.

Table I.2   Noticing insider-ness and outsider-ness

Indicators of My Insider-ness	Indicators of My Outsider-ness
If I find myself saying 'we' when I mean 'you'.	When I keep referring to 'your organization' or to examples and ideas from other organizations.
When I am copied into emails I don't expect to receive.	When I find I do not know who to contact or involve.
When I am expected to do something I have not contracted for, as if I am an employee or friend.	Feeling I can say what has to be said, however difficult, to whomever needs to hear it.
When concerns about success strongly influence my behaviour.	Knowing I can end this working relationship and survive/feel competent.
Being offered a reason for doing/not doing something that assumes my client's interests are my interests.	Realising I have little compassion for or interest in my client's fortunes.

These indicators are just that, a mix of behaviours, experiences and feelings that indicate my current insider-outsider status, according to my own perceptions and/or those of my client. They do not indicate whether my status is intrinsically positive or negative, as I hope is obvious. But operating at either end of the insider-outside index may give me cause for concern and invite me to pay more attention to the choices of role-taking available to me.

2   RISK TAKING

We are creatures of habit and routines and over time there is an accommodation between the roles expected of me and my sense of who I am and what I do 'in role'. I will 'adapt' to a role, 'identify with it, and obtain a sense of well being' from it (Czander 1993: 306). So it can be uncomfortable and feel alarming and risky when roles end unexpectedly or when expectations change about what constitutes a well worn role. Roles can function as transitional objects and offer comfort and reassurance, whether we love them or hate them. I experience risk when I step out from familiar roles and relationships where I know there is the opportunity for gain and the possibility of loss (Gephart 2009). If I decide to say 'No' to a valued internal client, I may lose my reputation *and* retain my integrity. Conversely, if I choose to be permanently available to my client (by taking phone calls on holiday or working all weekend) I might preserve my self-identity as martyr or buddy and risk undermining my authority with that client.

Authors in this book write about risk and power relations (Andrew Day), reputational risk (Karen Izod), living with the risk of transference and projection from their client (Pauline Holland), how clients can work hard to avoid risk taking (Sally R. Wigutow) and how insiders can become aware of and make sense of felt risk by paying attention to timing (Susan Whittle) and language. Victor O. Adebowale tuned into a phrase uttered by a manager that captured the risk facing his organization; that of 'Dining with the Devil'.

We tend to think of risk as less about opportunity and more about danger, the feeling that something bad will happen. This can become a perpetual preoccupation in high profile, project organizations where 'a perpetual Groundhog Day of keeping a low profile' (Stevens and Whittle: 78, in this book). Identifying how bad the risk might be, for whom, and in what circumstances is the business of risk management, which often uses the language of statistics and probability to defend against concerns of exposure and vulnerability. In her chapter on working as an associate, Karen Izod takes a different path to tell us how working with her client required '... giving up safer ways of doing things. In that sense, I had to be willing to bring a riskier version of myself, not just the person that I was perceived as being' (Izod: 159, in this book).

Theories of risk taking are contested (Hu et al. 2011) but boil down to 'How do different people decide what to worry about most?' (PERRI 6 2005: 93).

In my chapter on working with time, I wonder about the sorts of questions I might ask of myself and my client as indicators of the risks I am prepared to entertain, such as the risk of not delivering 'on time' because my client is not ready, or working to plan and risking failure. Which option evokes least discomfort, for me and for my client? Picking up on language and feelings can help risk assessment. For example, do I feel challenged, stressed, or bored (Carroll 2010)? Boredom is not an emotion usually associated with risk and we might expect to work hard to dissociate ourselves from boredom as something that others experience. But this dissociation goes to the heart of the not-me dimension of risk-taking and signals a level of discomfort and withdrawal that I may need to challenge.

The practice of organizational change, which involves choices about roles to be taken, the design of intervention strategies and the development of useful working relationships, aims to contain client anxieties arising from the agenda for change. Being clear about what's mine and what's the client's is a primary task for the change agent (Trist and Bamforth 1951). If the primary task is ambiguous or contested (perhaps because I am unsure of what to do or feel coerced into taking a particular role) then I am at risk of making the wrong choices. I may become hooked into the outcomes desired by my clients (improved processes; more effective people; less absenteeism; enhanced customer service or perhaps least hassle, no pain or no surprises) rather than helping my clients to work on *their* problems. This puts me at risk of choosing inappropriate roles, of designing ineffective intervention strategies, and of developing useless or perhaps counter-productive relationships. If I sense that not only is there room for making the wrong choices but that what needs to be worked on is unmanageable, then I am faced with what Hirschhorn calls 'the primary risk'. This is 'the felt risk of choosing the wrong primary task, that is, a task that ultimately cannot be managed' (Hirschhorn 1999: 9). To defend myself against the dread of this realization, I may suppress or deny my awareness of the impossibility of my primary task, which is to contain anxieties arising from the agenda for change. What follows is the very real possibility that I can become stuck in a practice space of working on tasks and taking up roles which, although designed to by-pass the risk of failure, make it inevitable, because I am not working on what's really needed.

Authors in this book encounter and cope with the felt risk of choosing something that cannot be managed or contained, the primary risk, in a number of ways. From his position of CEO, Victor O. Adebowale took up a role of internal consultant to help members of his organization confront and work with the risk of changing their corporate identity, from a charity to a business. The felt risk of this potentially impossible task is conveyed in his title: 'Dining with the Devil'. Naming the primary risk in this way perhaps helped members of his organization to contain some of their shared anxieties about what needed to be done. As consultant to family businesses, Sally R. Wigutow describes how a family avoided the risks to family relationships that might result from open discussion of preferences for succession, by sticking to the worries of daily operations (Wigutow: Chapter 6, in this book). Andrew Day's case highlights 'the challenges and risks for the internal OD Consultant in taking up a position in the existing power structures when the task is to work on power dynamics in the organization' (Day: 41, in this book).

If the felt risk is not contained, a group sense of risk can emerge and spread quickly, pushing task-directed work out of the way in favour of regressive defences. Bion's basic assumption groups are a collective defence against the perceived risk of not being able to do the work that needs to be done for the group to survive. (Bion 1961 and see Robin C. Stevens, Chapter 9 in this book, for a description of this phenomenon.) Group decisions can be more risky than decisions taken individually. This is referred to as 'risky shift' (Burnstein 1969) and is said to result from a lowered sense of personal responsibility or potential blame felt by an individual when there is collective decision making. Internal consultants and change agents and those practitioners working psychoanalytically are at particular risk of taking on group and organizational responsibilities as their own, as Pauline Holland warns:

> [I]f the consultants are not able, over time, to speak to the issues and organizational themes arising from their interventions with managers and teams, there is a real danger that they are left holding intense and painful emotions that they won't know what to do with. They risk getting caught up in the emotional undertow of the organization and becoming identified with the dissociative aspects of the emotional life of the organization. (Holland: 56, in this book)

Internal consultants and change agents are cultural artefacts of their organizations. So it's much more of a challenge for insiders to find ways to understand and work with their client's sense of risk without becoming subject to the prevailing risk culture (Walby and Doyle 2009). Constant vigilance is required to identify what I have learned to assume is risky and what I have learned to discount or not notice as risky, to both my organization and myself. Andrew Koehler offers an example of the difference between an insider and an outsider perspective on risk when he describes the work of a high security plutonium plant in the USA. Looking at the massive and intimidating external physical appearance of the plant, Koehler notices that, while an outsider might interpret the structure 'as evidence that plutonium handling is something worse than snake handling', to an insider the massive security is evidence 'of service being performed in the service of national policy' (Koehler 2002: 108–9).

3   RELATIONSHIPS

The preferred model for organizing has been changing for some time, from centralized control and dependable hierarchies to organizations configured through self-organized networks and social capital (Jung 2008). These loosely coupled (Alderfer 1980) models of organizing are thought to be more efficient than earlier, bureaucratic forms, both for picking up trends and reshaping work quickly. At the same time, clients are becoming more sophisticated in their selection and evaluation of consultants (Werr and Styhre 2003). Against this background, those in the business of organization change now need to develop 'relational agency'. This requires 'recognizing how others interpret and react to problems and aligning one's own interpretation and responses to take up roles of partners, collaborating with clients to craft bespoke interventions, rather than roles as priests, prophets, or the police of change' (Edwards 2010: 2).

But all too often, working on the consulting relationship can be seen as a 'necessary inconvenience', an unavoidable task to be attended to so that the real work of changes to strategy, structure and technology can steam ahead (Block 2000: xvi). Getting the relationship right is crucial because 'Consulting is primarily a relationship business' (Block 2000: 327). Relationships involve choices about how much of myself (if any) I bring to my work (Berg 2002) and whether my presentation of myself (Goffman 1969) is authentic or involves role playing and tactical positioning.

> *Occupational roles that allow for the presentation of 'oneself' or allow persons to be 'themselves' will lead to greater degrees of satisfaction. These are roles that offer a wider variety of behaviours and allow role occupants to integrate attributes of the role into their personality. (Czander 1993: 306)*

Authenticity is a high-risk strategy because I show myself (Block 2000: xvii). Pauline Holland describes her disappointment that all discussions with her client about implementing changes to organization design 'took place within the context of the line manager-direct report relationship' (Holland: 54, in this book). This made for a difficult working relationship and her role was reduced to 'a pair of hands' to the Director, rather than the more collaborative working relationship she had wanted and believed would be more effective. She had not dare risk negotiating a more collegial relationship. It's easy to become tired of, if not exhausted by, the incessant relationship building work that accompanies more collaborative forms of practice. From her role as an associate working on behalf of a host consulting firm, Karen Izod reveals that:

> *It can be tempting for associates to close off the boundary with the host organization: in effect, to work in a quasi-independent role with the client, so as to limit the need to position the intervention within the host organization and to protect one's self from what can feel like additional emotional work. (Izod: 147, in this book)*

Not challenging or taking-on client's assumptions about the working relationship is a constant danger that can hinder the scope and possibilities for organizational change. Working on the relationship between consultant and client may embody what needs to change organizationally in microcosm. In his case study of consulting to a manufacturing alliance from his role of internal OD consultant, Andrew Day writes:

> *[I] aligned myself with individuals who held power in the organization. Looking back now, I can see that I became so attuned to the power dynamics in the organization that I was unaware at times of how I participated in them. (Day: 24, in this book)*

He found that power relations were a recurrent theme throughout his consulting assignment.

How clients relate to their consultants, how groups relate to leaders, line mangers to advisers, and vice versa, can offer data helpful to the crafting of interventions to support organization change. Catching sight of the conventions that influence what is expected of whom and what is appropriate and inappropriate behaviour in the relationship, for both consultant and client, introduces the possibility of choice. Sally R. Wigutow felt a 'sense of self-righteousness' on behalf of her client who had been disrespected by her brother, an owner of the business. Sally was in touch with her own experiences of family and family business and was able to bring this aspect of herself to her work to offer insights about her client's problems. This does not mean that Sally acted-out her self-righteousness! Managing oneself in role so as to be in the relationship while not subject to the relationship is the tricky business of insider/outsider dynamics.

Overview of Chapters

We hope this book fills a gap in the market for a serious, conceptual and accessible book on the practice of organizational change from an insider perspective. Through their accounts, the authors enrich what we believe is an over-simplified and sterile conceptual split that pervades the literature on organizational change. This divides the world into two camps: change that is led from inside or change led from outside the client system. This book takes a more nuanced stance than the hokey-cokey model of putting your whole self in or your whole self out. We work with a continuum of insider-ness and outsider-ness. These are in dynamic tension and continuously shifting as concerns about boundaries, belonging, authority and identity arise in the course of working to change organizations. Being aware of these dynamics and their impact can help us to navigate our organizational spaces more effectively and work with client systems to illuminate organizational issues. For 'insiders' this means finding ways to step out occasionally and for 'outsiders' it can mean seeking ways to step further in. This feels risky. The challenge for both is finding ways to make use of their insider/outsider perspectives without becoming enmeshed in their client organization's regressive and inertial dynamics.

Writing about change in your own organization or in an organization where close relationships have developed is difficult, even threatening, and many consultants, executives and project leads feel the need to present the good news story or not write at all. My invitation to contributors was to risk writing about their practice in ways that would take readers into the difficulties and dilemmas encountered when changing organizations from within. For some, the risks were too great and they dropped out of the project. Those who have succeeded in contributing a chapter have struggled with what and how much to reveal; with how to convey what happened against presenting a self interested account; and with how they will be judged. Here is an outline of those chapters in the words of the authors.

CHAPTER 1 – ANDREW DAY, 'POWER AND THE INTERNAL: WORKING ON THE EDGE'

The practice of consulting can be conceptualized, in part, to be a political process as it involves the consultant engaging and participating in the power dynamics within the client system. From this position, I argue that individuals who are trying to bring about change from within an organization find themselves in a paradoxical position. To bring about change in the organization they need to work through its existing power structures while at the same time implicitly or explicitly challenging how power is configured. I explore this tension by describing and reflecting on my experience of working on an internal consulting project from when I worked as an Organization Development consultant for a global manufacturing business. Through the case, I describe how power dynamics and structures can be understood at different conceptual levels and how internals can work with power dynamics to bring about change from within an organization.

CHAPTER 2 – PAULINE HOLLAND, 'STRATEGIC MOMENTS IN INTERNAL CONSULTING: INTRODUCING FUNCTIONAL LEARNING ENVIRONMENTS IN A SOCIAL CARE ORGANIZATION'

As the social service organization I worked for expanded significantly in size and scope to become a substantial national operation, spans of control expanded to accommodate the growth, and middle managers became more outward-facing in order to secure and sustain funding from a very competitive external environment. Supervision – a model that balanced providing support with accountability – was replaced with 'business meetings' where key result areas were identified and monitored. The emotional world of work appeared to have been subjugated in favour of goals and targets. These changes often left frontline managers and their teams feeling unsupported in their difficult and challenging task. I write about my efforts as the new Training and Development Manager to address this need by trying to build a more sustainable 'functional learning environment' in which practitioners and managers could openly acknowledge and work with anxieties, uncertainties and risks inherent in the work.

CHAPTER 3 – VICTOR O. ADEBOWALE, 'DINING WITH THE DEVIL'

I tell my story of CEO as change agent from my position as CEO of a charity called CT, which was established in 1964 to deliver services to address substance misuse in people leaving the armed forces. From 1990 to 2001, CT significantly expanded its services; it also had four CEOs, each appointed to address issues relating to the need to cut costs while increasing income generated through fund-raising and grants from local government. When I arrived in 2001, CT was under severe strain as a result of dwindling fundraising income and increased competition for fewer grants. My brief was to devise a truly sustainable new business model and address the culture of 'them and us' between the leadership of CT and those outside of the paid executive team. This chapter explores my experience of change from the inside, without using the consulting relationship as a 'way out'.

CHAPTER 4 – ROBIN C. STEVENS AND SUSAN ROSINA WHITTLE, 'MANAGING PROJECTS: HOW AN ORGANIZATION DESIGN APPROACH CAN HELP'

This chapter describes how principles of organization design can be used to good effect in project management. Project management is classically thought of as control of scope, schedule and budget. This formulation is inadequate to describe the complexity of developing and delivering projects today, many of which require the involvement of multiple organizations and people from a range of professional disciplines and are buffeted by the turbulent economy. The chapter will draw on our experience of consulting to and leading projects (major construction, supply chain management, performance improvement, policy evaluation) to explore the dilemmas that project managers face, as insiders in temporary organizations, in orchestrating the complex constellation of people and factors that constitute project life. We will offer some ideas about containment rather than control as a descriptor of the role of project leaders.

CHAPTER 5 – SUSAN ROSINA WHITTLE, 'QUICK, QUICK, SLOW: TIME AND TIMING IN ORGANIZATIONAL CHANGE'

Much of the work of organizational consultants and change agents is time-centred: slowing down or speeding up decision-making; redesigning work to be just in time; challenging a longing for the past or a flight to the future; coping with can't-wait-crises arising from regime and regulation changes. How organizations relate to time is a fundamental aspect of their culture. Changing organizational routines and practices frequently involves changing this relationship and the thinking and behaviours informed by it. Without the containment of an explicit contract, insider consultants and change leaders may lose sight of or be unable to sustain time and activity boundaries in line with their plans for organizational change. Drawing on my experiences of providing professional development programs and shadow consulting to insider consultants and change leaders over 20 years, I describe: how orchestrating and responding to the tempo of organizational change is a core competence for insider consultants and change leaders; why this competence is difficult to learn by doing, as insiders are artefacts of their organizations; what to look for to diagnose a tempo problem; some tools and techniques that can help insiders to tussle with the tempo of planned organizational change by interrupting rhythms and harmonizing participation.

CHAPTER 6 – SALLY R. WIGUTOW, 'FAMILY BUSINESS: INSIDE AND OUTSIDE THE SYSTEMS AT PLAY'

Several years ago when a colleague hired me to work with him in a family business in which the entrepreneur's life stage and her organization's stage of development were not aligned, we found ourselves enmeshed in the family's dynamics, trying to manage the boundaries of family and organization – *insiders in the organization, outsiders in the family and sometimes the reverse.* Work in or with a family business takes place within a multi-faceted system imbued with the history of a particular family; it usually holds all the triggers necessary for emotional response on the part of each participant, family and non-family alike. Being able to look at the inherent tensions and overlaps in the family, business and governance systems to understand their impact on work and family is a large part of an organizational consultation to family-owned enterprises. I delineate models I have found useful to understanding organizational dilemmas in this domain and offer vignettes from my practice to illustrate and make links between them.

CHAPTER 7 – LISA GARDINER, ELIZABETH SUMMERS AND GERHARD RAFTL, 'BY INVITATION ONLY?'

We work as a relational consultancy because it provides valuable opportunities to positively influence practice in organizations. As with the laws of physics, the position and other properties of objects are only meaningful in relation to other objects. Also, well-regarded relationships are characterized by a level of depth and longevity, allowing both parties to experience changes in capacity built through positive reciprocal action. This approach requires the organization to invite us inside and allow us to see and experience areas of strength and vulnerability. We use a case study to describe how positioning clinical and organizational consultants physically inside the organization can make a difference to the outcome of interventions and how mirroring client and organizational behaviour can assist consultants to gain a deeper understanding and work more effectively with organizations experiencing distress or chaos.

CHAPTER 8 – KAREN IZOD, 'TOO CLOSE FOR COMFORT? ATTENDING TO BOUNDARIES IN ASSOCIATE RELATIONSHIPS'

This chapter explores the issues relating to consulting identities that are generated in working across the boundary of an organization as an associate consultant. The primary contention is that associative relationships are formed on the basis of identifying with, or being in agreement with some aspect of the host organization, that is, its principles, the way it does business, its theoretical stance. But inherent in this formulation are the dynamics of difference, that is, how to manage aspects of the association that are to do with separateness and autonomy. I will offer examples from my own practice as an associate consultant and as shadow consultant to others practicing as associates to explore these relationships, trying to bring in the client's voice where possible. Key lenses to analyze these vignettes will be trust and control as aspects of power relations, identity and belonging, and organization in the mind. Contracting as transactional and relational activities which influence the nature of authority that the consultant can assume are central considerations.

CHAPTER 9 – ROBIN C. STEVENS, 'THEORY FOR SKILLED PRACTITIONERS'

The tales from the field in this book are purposefully short of the citations found in academic articles. We think that our on-the-ground stories of the dilemmas of our consulting work offer other practitioners rich help in making sense of their own experiences. But theory does in fact underpin what the practitioners who have shared their work in this book, all of whom practice in the systems psychodynamics tradition, do. Accordingly, we thought that it would be useful to include a chapter that summarizes some of the theories important to this tradition: organizations as systems; dynamics of collaboration and intergroup relationships; key psychodynamic concepts, especially how they illuminate the dynamics of groups; reflective practice; the nature of change; and organizational design.

References

Alderfer, C.P. 1980. Consulting to underbounded systems, in *Advances in Experiential Social Processes*, edited by C.P. Alderfer and C.L. Cooper. Volume 2, New York: Wiley, 267–95.

Argyris, C. 1970. *Intervention Theory and Method*. Reading, MA: Addison-Wesley.

Bateson, G. 1972. *Steps to an Ecology of Mind*. Chicago, IL: Chicago University Press.

Berg, David N. 2002. Bringing one's self to work: A Jew reflects. *The Journal of Applied Behavioral Science*, 38(4), 397–415.

Bion, W. 1961. *Experiences in Groups and Other Papers*. London: Tavistock Publications.

Block, P. 1981. *Flawless Consulting: A Guide to Getting Your Expertise Used*. New York: Jossey-Bass/Pfeiffer.

Boggs, J.S. and Rantisi, N.M. 2003. The relational turn in economic geography. *Journal of Economic Geography*, 3, 109–16.

Burnstein, E. 1969. An analysis of group decisions involving risk ('the risky shift'). *Human Relations*, 22(5), 381–95.

Caldwell, R. 2003. Models of change agency: A fourfold classification. *British Journal of Management*, 14(2), 131–42.

Carroll, B.J., Parker, P. and Inkson, K. 2010. Evasion of boredom: An unexpected spur to leadership? *Human Relations*, 63(7), 1031–49.

Cheung-Judge, M-Y. 2001. The self as an instrument – A cornerstone for the future of OD. *OD Practitioner*, 33(3),

Goffman, E. 1969. *The Presentation of Self in Everyday Life*. London: The Penguin Press.

Holland, P. 2013. Strategic moments in internal consulting: Introducing functional learning environments in a social care organization. Chapter 2 in this book.

Hu, S., Blettner, D. and Bettis, R.A. 2011. Adaptive aspirations: Performance consequences of risk preferences at extremes and alternative reference groups. *Strategic Management Journal*, 32, 1426–36.

Czander, W. 1993. *The Psychodynamics of Work and Organization*. New York: Guildford Press.

Edwards, A. 2010. *Being an Expert Professional Practitioner: The Relational Turn in Expertise (Professional and Practice-based Learning)*. London: Springer.

Ganesh, S.R. 1978. Organizational consultants: A comparison of styles. *Human Relations*, 31(1), 1–28.

Gephart, R.P., Van Maanen, J. and Oberlechner, T. 2009. Organizations and risk in late modernity. *Organization Studies*, 30(2), 141–55.

Havelock, R.G. 1973. *The Change Agent's Guide to Innovation in Education*. Englewood Cliffs, NJ: Educational Technology Publications.

Heron, J. 2001. *Helping the Client*. 5th Edition. London: Sage Publications.

Hirschhorn, L. 1999. The primary risk. *Human Relations*, 52(1), 5–23.

Hoyle, L. 2004. From sycophant to saboteur – responses to organizational change, in *Working Below the Surface: The Emotional Life of Contemporary Organizations*, edited by Huffington, C., Halton, W. and Hoyle, L. London: Karnac Books, 87–106.

Izod, K. 2009. How does a turn towards relational thinking influence consulting practice in organizations and groups? in *Object Relations and Social Relations*, edited by Clarke, S., Hahn, H. and Hoggett, P. London: Karnac Books.

Jung, N. 2008. Do Clients Really Become More 'Professional'? Analyzing Clients' New Ways of Managing Consultants. [Online]. Available at: http://ssrn.com/abstract=1440684 [accessed: 31 May 2012].

Kitay, J. and Wright, C. 2003. Expertise and organizational boundaries: Roles of Australian management consultants. *Asia Pacific Business Review*, 9(3), 21–40.

Koehler, A. 2002. Defining risk and safety in a high security organization: Bunkering at the Los Alamos Plutonium Handling Facility, in *Constructing Risk and Safety in Technological Practice*, edited by Berner, B. and Summerton, J. London: Routledge, 106–17.

Krantz, J.S. and Maltz, M. 1997. A framework for consulting to organizational role. *Consulting Psychology Journal: Practice and Research*, 49(2), 137–51.

Lacey, M. 1995. Internal consulting: Perspectives on the process of planned change. *Journal of Organizational Change Management*, 8(3), 75–84.

Miller, E.J. and Rice, A.K. 1967. *Systems of Organization*. London: Tavistock Publications.

Ottaway, R.N. 1983. The change agent: A taxonomy in relation to the change process. *Human Relations*, 36(4), 361–92.

PERRl 6 2005. What's in a frame? Social organization, risk perception and the sociology of knowledge. *Journal of Risk Research*, 8(2), 91–118.

Schein, E. 1988. *Process Consultation Volume 1: Its role in OD*. Reading, MA: Addison Wesley Publishing.

Schein, E. 1998. *Process Consulting Revisited: Building the Helping Relationship*. Reading, MA: Addison Wesley Longman.

Stevens, R. and Whittle, S.R. 2012. Managing projects: How an organization design approach can help. Chapter 4 in this book.

Sturdy, A.J., Wylie, N. and Wright, C. 2010. *Management Consultancy without Consulting Firms or Consultants*. Paper presented at European Group for Organizational Studies Colloquium, Lisbon, June 28–30, 2010.

The Association for Psychodynamic Practice and Counseling in Organizational Settings. [Online]. Available at: http://appcios.com/our-approach/why-psychodynamic/ [accessed: 31 May 2012].

Tichy, N.M. 1975. How different types of change agent diagnose organizations. *Human Relations*, 23(5), 771–9.

Trist, E. and Bamforth, W. 1951. Some social and psychological consequences of the long wall method of coal-getting. *Human Relations*, 4, 3–38.

Ulrich, D. 1997. *Human Resource Champions: The Next Agenda for Adding Value and Delivering Results*. Boston, MA: Harvard Business School Press.

Walby, K. and Doyle, Aron. 2012. Their risks are my risks: On shared risk epistemologies, including altruistic fear for companion animals. [Carleton University Sociological Research Online]. Available at: http://www.socresonline.org.uk/14/4/3.html [accessed: 21 May 2012].

Werr, A. and Styhre, A. 2003. Management consultants – friend or foe? Understanding the ambiguous client-consultant relationship. *International Studies of Management and Organization*, 32(4), 43–66.

Whittle, S.R. 2009. Introduction: The challenge of a mind-ful approach to organizational consulting, in *Mind-ful Consulting*, edited by Whittle, S.R. and Izod, K.. London: Karnac Books, xxi–xxxiii.

Wright, C. 2009. Inside out? Organizational membership, ambiguity and the ambivalent identity of the internal consultant. *British Journal of Management*, 20(3), 309–22

1

Power and the Internal: Working on the Edge

Andrew Day

> *Power is anything that tends to render immobile and untouchable those things that are offered to us as real, as true, as good. (Foucault 1988: 1)*

I consider the practice of organization consulting to be in essence a political process as it is influenced by and influences the distribution of power in an organization. Consultants participate in these processes in their client systems and cannot stand outside of them. My intention in this chapter is to explore this aspect of internal consulting by examining how internals can understand and work with power dynamics in organizations. If we look a little closer, we can see that much of what we do as consultants is associated with questions of power, for instance:

- Who can authorize me to take up my role in the system and for what purpose?

- Who will pay for my time and what do they expect in return? If I am an internal, how will my contributions be recognized? What limits do I put on my involvement?

- Who will be involved in the consultation and whose interests will be considered?

- How do I understand the underlying issues and how might my account and that of others be contested?

- Who wants change, in what form and for what purpose? How will such desires be resisted and by whom?

- How will changes be brought about and who will be involved?

- Who will and how will my work be evaluated?

In most organizations, however, power is rarely questioned or openly explored. Moreover, individuals tend to discount their own political motives and behaviour while describing others' behaviour as 'being political'. This challenges the consultant to make decisions about how to make sense of and work with power. It presents a dilemma as to whether to act in a manner that maintains the existing power dynamics or seeks to disturb them. This is the line of enquiry that I wish to pursue in this chapter. Firstly, by considering how we can understand and work with power as consultants, and secondly by reflecting on my experience of power dynamics when I worked as an internal.

Power Dynamics and the Internal

Earlier in my career, I worked for eight years as an internal Organizational Development consultant in a large global multinational manufacturing business. Over this period, I developed a rich and subtle understanding of how power was enacted in the organization and how to navigate sensitive political relationships. This is one of the primary advantages of internal consultants in comparison with externals (Scott 2008). While achieving insight into the power dynamics, I was also aware that my interests tended to be dependent on how I connected with and aligned myself with individuals who held power in the organization. Looking back now, I can see that I became so attuned to the power dynamics in the organization that I was unaware at times of how I participated in them. On reflection, I was trying to balance a distinctive identity as a practitioner while being accepted as an 'insider' who had access to formal and informal networks. I could not rely on my position in the hierarchy for authority and like most internals I had to rely on my professional credibility and internal relationships as a source of power (Wright 2009).

To take up their role, internals are challenged to maintain a marginal position which requires them to operate at the edge and on the boundary of the organization (Scott 2008). I experienced this to be a constant struggle. To influence change, I often found myself working through the existing power structures, yet paradoxically my practice often involved an implicit or explicit challenge to how power was configured in the organization. This paradoxical position is, I believe, central to the internal role. In the case I explore below, it appears in multiple relationships throughout the consulting assignment.

A FRAMEWORK FOR UNDERSTANDING POWER

The concept of power is 'essentially contested' (Lukes 1974: 14). It remains ambiguous, abstract and elusive (Eriksen 2001). Yet in spite of this, I believe it is a valuable concept as it provides a conceptual link between the person and the group, and the individual and society. It helps us understand who may do what, where and in what ways in a given social context.

In my practice I conceptualize power to be operating at three related yet distinct levels. These are the levels of: social structures, relational process and intra-psychic dynamics. Table 1.1 below describes the three conceptual levels

Table 1.1   The different conceptual levels of power

	Conceptual Level of Power		
	Social Structure	**Relational Process**	**Intra-psychic Dynamics**
Nature of power.	A resource or capacity.	Embedded in and immanent to relationships	Subjective states of powerfulness and powerlessness.
Form.	Overt, covert and latent conflicts between interests.	The social rules and boundaries that enable and constrain action.	Internalized images of self and other.
Where power is present.	Unequally distributed across the social structure and across different individuals and groups in society.	Dispersed across relational networks.	In the images and fantasies that we hold of authority figures.
Core assumptions.	Power is a thing that is possessed by individuals.	Power reflects the interdependence between individuals.	Our unconscious shapes our experience of power and authority.
What is revealed?	Conflicts of interest and the exclusion of groups from decisions.	The dynamic and contextually specific presence of power at every level of the organization.	The emotional and unconscious dynamics behind power relations.
Critique or limitations.	An emphasis on social structure can be overly deterministic overlooking the role of agency and choice.	Downplays the role of economic, technological and political resources in the exercising of power.	Downplays the role of social structures and processes in limiting the opportunities and choices of the individual.

and summarizes briefly how the sociological, political and psychological theory conceptualizes each level.

Power as a Social Structure

Structural accounts of power emphasize how power arises from the relatively fixed aspect of the social structure of societies and organizations within them. Power is formed by the tacit and taken-for-granted basis of the social order which becomes legitimized through the use of symbols, language, rituals and normative assumptions (Pfeffer 1981). As such, differences in power become embedded in the fabric of society. This results in the social stratification of groups within societies and the unequal distribution of social status, privilege and materials on a systematic basis (Crompton 1993).

Marxists and feminists have observed how these structures tend to be organized along class, racial and gender divisions. Power is inextricably linked therefore to socio-political identity groups. As practitioners, we need to be aware of how our position in society has shaped and influenced our identity, view of the world and others. I am white, British, middle class, male and professionally educated. My life history is not therefore an experience of being oppressed, marginalized or discriminated against. I have experienced power from a position of privilege and opportunity which will be reflected no doubt in my consulting practice. You, the reader, may well see ways in which my position in society shapes how I engage with power in the case I present below.

Structural accounts define power to be the ability to get others to do what you want them to, if necessary against their will (Weber 1978) or to get them to do something they otherwise would not (Dahl 1957). The assumption being that power is a capacity or resource that is possessed by individuals. Sources of power include: information, expertise, credibility, control of rewards, status and access to influential individuals (French and Ravens 1968). This perspective highlights the role of political elites, political coalitions and organized interest groups, such as unions and professional bodies, in organizations.

The structural perspective draws our attention to how actors in organizations exercise power to further their interests when they conflict with others' interests. This is most visible during periods of overt conflict or power struggles in an organization. Lukes (1974) observes that power can be exercised in more hidden or subtle forms. He argued that it can be used covertly to prevent the interests of specific groups from being represented or considered in decisions. This involves either the mobilization of bias (Bachrach and Baratz 1970) to shape decisions or the prevention of decisions from being discussed or acknowledged publically. He also draws attention to how power can be used to prevent overt and covert conflict from arising in the first place. In this form, power is used to shape the consciousness of others such that they come to accept the existing social order either because they see others' interests as being their own or they are not able to identify their own interests. For Lukes (1974: 24) this is 'the most effective and insidious use of power' as it leads to what Marxists have termed 'false consciousness' and 'alienation' whereby conflicts remain at a latent level. What are the implications for practice?

- Organizational development is likely to require the formal exercising of power by individuals in positions of authority to make decisions and legitimize forms of organization change. The internal consultant's influence and authority is frequently dependent on the degree of support that they receive from individuals who hold power and authority in the organization. As such, we become implicated in the existing structures of power and if we are not simply to reinforce the existing structures to further our own interests, we need to take a critical stance on our positioning in the established structures.

- Changes to organizational practices will give rise to overt, covert and latent conflicts between different interest groups in the organization as power structures shift. Conflicts will also reflect fears and vulnerability around real or potential losses of power. The internal consultant will need to make decisions about how, when and whether to facilitate the exploration of such conflicts.

- Planned and emergent change often requires consultants to involve individuals and groups that have previously been excluded from formal and informal decision-making processes. The internal consultant will need to make decisions as to when and how to bring different voices into negotiations and decision-making processes that relate to the change processes.

Power as a Relational Process

A relational perspective highlights how power is not simply held by specific individuals or groups but is present at every level and sphere of life, affecting the powerful and the powerless. It reveals the dialectic nature of power relations whereby the balance of power is held *between* individuals rather than by them (Giddens 1984). For every act of power we can also expect to find forms of resistance or acts that work against it (Foucault 1980). Power is therefore dynamic, constantly shifting and, at times, paradoxical. It is an inevitable outcome of living together and interdependence (Elias 1978).

Power relations represent the social boundaries that constrain and enable action (Hayward 1998; Elias 1978). They are inscribed within the contextual 'rules of the game' (Clegg 1975) and are played out through the strategies and skills that actors exercise in the enactment of them. Power dynamics revolve around the processes of inclusion and exclusion (Elias 1978) as groupings are formed through social interactions. This gives rise to an 'Us' and a 'Them'. For me, paying attention to power dynamics highlights how formal and informal relationships enable action and change, while in doing so they necessarily exclude people who are outside of specific social connections or groupings.

Power is enacted through social discourse whereby different actors position themselves in relation to others according to their status and identity. We typically experience this process in the form of status games that are played out in groups and interpersonal relationships. Power can also be equated to claims to knowledge (Foucault 1972). Different discourses and ideologies represent bodies of knowledge which form the basis of social practices (Foucault 1972). Foucault (1980) observed how 'regimes of truth' – unquestioned patterns of discourse – are established in society to create our reality. These 'regimes of truth' become a means of preserving the current social order by making it seem natural and unquestionable.

Power as a relational process brings into view the taken-for-granted, tactical and unobtrusive presence of power in the interactions between multiple agents in a social system. It illuminates how power arises through relationships *with* others and moves towards power residing on the consent of others (Hindess 1996). What are the implications for practice?

- Social boundaries and the implicit 'rules of the game' put limits on what forms of action are acceptable in organizations. If different social rules are to emerge, then the internal consultant will need to find ways of helping a client system become aware of how they enable and constrain different forms of action. This is likely to require the questioning of dominant patterns of discourse and what is presented as *right and normal* and what is seen as *wrong* and *deviant*.

- The nature and form of problems and issues experienced by a client system will be contested between different groups and individuals. The internal consultant will need to make decisions as to how they raise and question different accounts and positions in a manner that does not result in them being excluded by influential parties.

- Creative and generative forms of power will involve groups of people coming together to negotiate how they can work together to achieve outcomes that they could not achieve individually. This is likely to require the internal consultant to work both through formal and informal relationships to develop common ground and consensus amongst different actors.

Intra-psychic Dynamics of Power

Psychodynamic theory argues that how we engage with authority figures and exercise our power reflects our unconscious, internal world. Both Freud and Lacan took the position that the family, society, gender and each of our lives are constructed on the premise that power is unequally distributed. We are all highly ambivalent about power, as a result of the struggles that we encounter with early authority figures. These early relational experiences give rise to internalized images of benign or punitive authority (Hirschhorn 1988) which shape how we experience power relations in our later lives.

Our internalized images of authority can be evoked when we encounter authority or take up a position of authority. We often project benign or punitive images onto individuals in positions of authority. This shapes how we participate in power relations, our sense of personal authority and experience of authority figures. We may therefore perceive individuals in power as being critical of us, aggressive, lacking in some way or in contrast we may idealize them and see them as all powerful. Our images of authority can give rise to beliefs and fantasies as to what we are able and permitted to do in our roles or the extent to which we need to feel controlled by or in control of others. They can often lead to pejorative judgements of individuals in positions of power or those who are perceived to stand in opposition. When holding positions of authority we can equally project onto others and assume that they may hold the same images of ourselves as we hold of authority figures. This can prevent us from taking up our role and authority.

Our own narcissistic process can lead us to feel omnipotent or impotent in our work with clients, believing we are either all powerful or powerless. Consultants and leaders are prone to both hubris and helplessness and to despair in their roles. These polarized positions arise from the vulnerabilities and fantasies of the role holder and projections from the client system. In my practice, I can find myself acting on the belief that I can change the organization or, in contrast, believing that I am utterly powerless to make any difference in my role. Neither position is helpful to either myself or my client, although, if I can tolerate and explore my response, I may be able to reach an understanding of my reactions. From this perspective, the challenge to the internal consultant is to remain grounded by staying in touch with one's capabilities and with the limits of what is possible in a given context. What are the implications for practice?

- Primitive emotions, such as envy, aggression or fear, tend to get projected onto individuals at the top and bottom of power distributions. The internal consultant as a figure of authority is also likely to be a recipient of such projections from others. Consultants need to tolerate and contain such projections if they are to support individuals and groups to work through the emotional material that relates to the consulting task.

- Internal consultants need to find ways of containing the anxieties and vulnerabilities of individuals and groups to help them to own their projections. This enables individuals to constructively negotiate and assert their interests during periods of organizational change. In order to facilitate this process, internal consultants will need to be able to take up their authority, clarify roles and hold boundaries.

CASE STUDY: EXPERIENCES AND REFLECTIONS ON POWER AS AN INTERNAL

This case describes my experience of power dynamics in an internal consulting project. At the time I was working in the role I referred to earlier in the chapter. I have referred to the organization as Global Corp (GC) to protect its identity and have chosen not to name individuals who were involved. In the case, I have described my experience of power dynamics at each of the three levels and discussed how power shaped the consulting work.

In the spirit of this chapter, I want to acknowledge that as the author I have the power to construct a narrative that portrays others and myself in a particular light. I have chosen not to comment on interpersonal dynamics, as I do not have the other person's account to supplement my own. This is most apparent in my decision not to describe in detail the relationship with my colleague at the time. Our relationship was for the most part collaborative and collegial. My reflections are based on my personal experiences of power dynamics in the client system and interview material and discussions with people in the organization at the time of the work.

The remit of my role was to provide consulting support to GC's European Business Unit. I reported into the Head of Learning and Development who reported into the Vice President for HR. The European Business Unit was one of several large business units (BU) within GC's complex global divisional structure.

The consulting assignment involved making recommendations for changing the internal governance structures of an alliance between GC and another global manufacturer, International Corp. (IC). The alliance made use of the engineering capabilities of both firms to design and produce engines. These were used by each of the five BUs inside GC and by IC to assemble their core products. Figure 1.1 below depicts the organizational boundaries for the alliance, showing both those inside of GC and some of the relevant boundaries within IC. A small management team was responsible for representing the

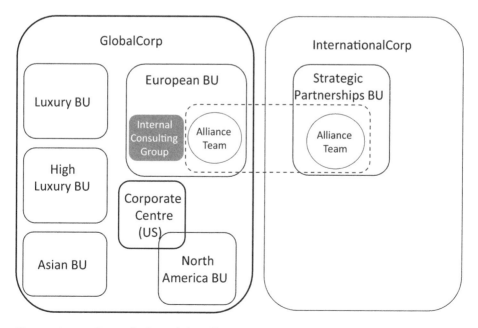

Figure 1.1   **Boundaries of the alliance**

interests of GC in the alliance with IC. On a day to day basis they worked with a team inside IC, who were part of its Strategic Partnerships Directorate. The Vice-President of this group reported directly into the Chairman for IC.

Entry and Contracting

The initiator of the project was the CEO for the European Business Unit. Through a conversation with the Head of HR, he made a request for myself and a colleague to take on the project. We had just finished another piece of work for him and he felt that some of the learning from it could be applied to the alliance. He wanted us to work with its management team to help them make improvements to the governance processes. We knew little about either the alliance or the managers who represented GC's participation in it.

In our initial conversations with the alliance managers, they explained that inside GC the alliance was perceived to be not meeting its performance targets. They believed this resulted from the inability of the BUs inside GC to agree what they wanted from the alliance. They felt that the BUs criticized any decisions managers made and rejected their proposals. The two alliance managers felt they were in an untenable situation. They were caught between differing agendas within GC and subjected to complaints from IC that GC was unwilling to commit to decisions that they thought had been agreed. They felt both their management and their partners expected them to fix the problems, but they did not feel they had the authority to address what needed to be changed.

Reflections on Power Relations

The project was assigned to us through the hierarchy by the CEO of our business unit. We complied with the assumption that we would take on the project without any questions or by explicitly negotiating our role with the CEO. Looking back now, this was partly as a result of some naivety on our part about the size and political complexity of the project. It also reflected our assumed position in the hierarchy which led us to be overly compliant with his request and our management's desire to acquiesce to his expectations. We were also seduced, I believe, by the status that was inferred through the personal request of the CEO.

Our point of entry into the system was towards the bottom of the power structures inside GC. We could have taken up a more influential role in the situation if we had negotiated a contract with the CEO directly. This would have given us an opportunity to understand his agenda, the boundaries of the project as he perceived them and importantly, to secure his support for engaging his peers in the other BUs and the corporate leadership.

First Consultancy Cycle

The consulting work involved several cycles of planned change (Kolb and Frohman 1970). In the first cycle, we worked with the two alliance managers to explore their perceptions of the governance processes and to uncover what, in their opinion, was contributing to the frustrations and perceptions of ineffectiveness. On the basis of these discussions, we mapped the primary decision-making forums within GC, the interfaces between GC and IC and described the presenting problem as they understood it.

The alliance had grown rapidly in response to growth in demand for its products. This necessitated more complex strategic and operational decisions, which had significant long-term consequences for each of the partners and each of the business units inside GC. The alliance management team struggled to reach agreements for critical decisions between the business units inside GC. Each of the business units made different and competing demands on the alliance management, particularly around the specification and design of its products. Where decisions were made, the BUs perceived them to be in the interests of IC or the European BU.

The alliance managers felt politically out manoeuvred by their counterparts inside IC. They perceived them to be devious and manipulative. They observed that their counterparts in IC were able to use their relationship with the Chairman of their company to raise sensitive issues with the Chairman of GC. This reflected the simpler structure of IC and the direct access that they had to their Chairman via the VP of Strategic Partnerships for IC. They were particularly critical of the Group VP for Strategy for GC who reported into the Chairman. They felt he took IC's criticisms at face value and would take their side in political disputes. His behaviour probably reflected the desire of the Chairman of GC to maintain harmonious relations with IC because of the long term strategic importance of the alliance to GC. The alliance managers however felt exposed in the internal political dynamics within GC.

Many of the issues raised by the alliance managers reflected the power and political relations that emerged around the complex decisions and non-decision-making between representatives from the different organizations. Mutual distrust was undermined by hostile projections between the different parties and covert and overt political behaviour to protect their interests. Individuals or groups who were perceived as being powerful were presumed to be acting manipulatively or out of self-interest.

Reflections on Power Relations

In our interactions with the alliance management team we were left feeling overwhelmed, powerless and uncertain of how to proceed. They talked about the problems 'as if' the capacity to bring about change was located in senior managers above them in the hierarchy. Implicitly they discounted their capacity to influence the situation. We started to experience their anxiety about the politics of the situation and their feelings of powerlessness.

Looking back, we over-identified with their fears of the aggressive and hostile political relations at senior levels of the business. This left us feeling that the assignment was risky. We were also concerned as to how the representatives from the other business units would judge our loyalties, given our position as consultants within the European BU.

The Second Consultancy Cycle: Exploring Interests and Political Tensions

To understand the difficulties with reaching decisions, we met with each of the key political figures to understand their perceptions of the alliance's purpose and its governance processes. This helped us to understand how perspectives on the alliance differed and how this influenced decision-making processes.

Together with the alliance managers, we met with the Product Development VP for GC and the CEOs and Product Development VPs of each of the business units. The alliance managers did not want to involve the Chairman of GC or the VP for Strategy or any representatives from IC in our enquiry. They were anxious that the management of the European BU would feel exposed if they were involved given their position above them in GC's hierarchy. Their exclusions from the process could be seen as a political act to ensure that the interests of the European BU were protected and any blame or criticism would be directed towards either IC or the other BUs.

The meetings highlighted competing strategic debates (Holti 2002) and political tensions between the different business units within GC around the purpose and effectiveness of the alliance. The leadership of each of the business units did not agree on the alliance's strategic direction. These underlying tensions around strategic interests were not publically acknowledged or discussed. The Luxury and High Luxury business units wanted the products from the alliance to help them manufacture a differentiated, high specification product. Every other business unit wanted a specification that would enable it to compete on cost. To protect their independence, the North American, Luxury and High Luxury BUs retained their own manufacturing capacity for the product. Each of the business units argued they needed to protect their own interests because they could not trust IC, which was perceived to value cost differentiation rather than product differentiation. This reflected the BUs' worries about becoming too dependent on IC and the other BUs.

The BUs' leadership were frustrated and felt helpless as to how they could ensure the alliance met their needs. No group had overall dominance. It was contested as to who spoke for whom and with what authority. The existing governance structures within GC did not support the exploration and resolution of cross-business unit decisions for the alliance. The alliance managers had to therefore mediate between individual managers in the different business units in an ad hoc and political manner to reach decisions.

The business units expressed considerable ambivalence about the alliance. They thought of themselves as separate businesses and wanted to protect their historical independence. This was amplified by their perceived inability to influence or stop key decisions when they were not in line with their strategic interests. The relationships between the representatives of each of the business units were characterized by mistrust, hostility and suspicion. These processes were undermining collaboration.

Projections of incompetence were directed towards the alliance managers. They were of lower status in the hierarchy of GC and often found themselves blamed for the problems. They attempted to defend themselves and argued they did not have the authority to make critical decisions. This heightened their feelings of powerlessness and vulnerability.

We concluded that the alliance could be understood as an 'underbounded' system (Alderfer 1980). Its goals and purpose were unclear, and it involved multiple and competing authority relations and roles. This led to difficulties in determining who could and should meet. The inter-group dynamics were dominated by Fight–Flight (Bion 1961) whereby members act 'as if' they must flee from the threats they represent for each other or they engage in persistent unproductive conflict (Alderfer 1980). We framed the consulting task as being one of enabling the different representatives of GC to draw up clear boundaries around the task system by agreeing the key decisions that needed to be made, positions of authority, and leadership roles.

Reflections on Power Relations

We found ourselves confronted with a dilemma. In the absence of good enough authority and leadership structures in the client system, what was our authority to work with the system to address these issues? As internal consultants within a sub-system of the whole, what legitimacy did we have with representatives from the business units outside of our own? We did not feel we had permission from our own management to engage more senior managers from outside of our business unit. We came up against the power structures, those implicit rules of interaction. These did not permit employees from lower in the hierarchy to raise contentious or sensitive issues with higher levels of hierarchy without first obtaining their consent. As such, our position had started to mirror that of the alliance managers. Our task as internals was to find creative ways of working within the existing 'rules of the game' to engage the critical political figures in the consulting process while not alienating ourselves from our management. This seems to reflect the paradoxical role of the internal – how to work with existing power relations while simultaneously bringing them into question.

Third Cycle of Consulting: Feeding Back and Negotiating Change

The two alliance managers were very anxious at the end of these meetings as they felt they needed to make some proposals as to how the alliance could be more effectively managed inside GC to re-establish their credibility. We worked with them and the operational teams for the alliance to develop change proposals and options for a governance structure inside GC that would facilitate both strategic and operational decision-making. The proposed changes included: clarifying responsibilities for leading the alliance inside GC, identifying the key decisions and which representatives would need to meet to make them, identifying critical interfaces with IC and clarifying options for managing these interfaces, the establishment of a relationship manager role to act as the primary interface with IC, and the inclusion of senior representatives from the other business units in the steering committee for the alliance. We also recommended that the business units within GC undertake a strategic review to agree their long term needs for the alliance.

In this final cycle, together with the alliance managers, we went back to the senior managers in each of the business units to explore our proposals. We felt it was too risky and pragmatically difficult to get them together as a group. We hypothesized that this would stir up too much anxiety which would heighten the competitive power dynamics between the different business units. We therefore chose to meet separately with each of them to contain their level of anxiety (Winnicott 1971) and that of the alliance managers.

The alliance managers were anxious to meet first with the CEO and VP for Engineering in the European BU before speaking to the other business units. They also argued that one of the business units should be consulted only at the end of the process because they would 'be political' and want to build their own products. They did not want to involve the representatives from the Corporate Centre, namely the Chairman or Strategy VP for GC. In these responses, they discounted their own political behaviour while seeing those who held views contrary to their own as being political. We challenged their desire to secure support from their management before engaging the other stakeholders; however, pushing them to take greater political risks increased their anxiety and reluctance to act. We chose therefore to support them in briefing their direct managers and raise the question of how to involve the representatives from the other BU's. In this form, the feedback meetings became a political process with respect to who was involved and in which order. Figure 1.2, on the following page, below shows the order of the meetings as they took place across the formal hierarchy of the business.

We framed our observations and proposals in neutral, rational, analytical language to minimize the risks of playing into splits and igniting political sensitivities. We therefore emphasized the legitimate strategic concerns of each business unit and proposed a range of options for a cadence of decision-making forums inside GC where the key strategic and operational issues could be debated and understood. Our references to the hostility and the covert political behaviour were limited to observations that the underlying strategic debates and fears of losing control of their interests undermined mutual trust between the business units. Our framing of the issues in logical and factual terms enabled the different stakeholders to acknowledge the underlying tensions and

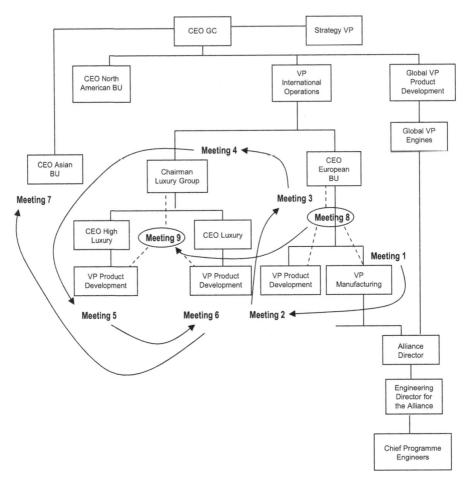

Figure 1.2   The order of the feedback meetings across the formal hierarchy

struggles. Our proposals presented different possibilities for how they could exercise their power and by expressing the possibilities as their choices, gave them a greater sense of agency.

The hostility and distrust of all of the different parties resurfaced in the feedback meetings. The CEO of the European BU was critical of the alliance management team but acknowledged the underlying problems with the governance processes. The senior managers from across the business units were united by their common interest in not being 'out-manoeuvred' by IC in the decision-making process. They individually agreed they needed to meet together to confirm what they each wanted from the alliance and how they communicated with the Chairman of GC around his role in managing the interface with IC. Each of the business units expressed a desire to have a 'voice' in the decision-making processes for the alliance.

The feedback meetings took nearly six months to complete because of the alliance managers' cautiousness in setting up meetings before they understood their BU's position on the issues that had surfaced during the enquiry. The initial meetings were with individuals who the alliance managers believed would support their proposals and the final meetings brought together the VPs for Product Development in each of the business units to agree the final proposals. These final meetings resulted in a shared acknowledgement of the problems with the existing governance structures and a commitment to work together to implement the proposed changes. Through the course of these meetings, a new governance structure was negotiated and agreed by the senior managers in each of the business units.

A review six months after the end of our work revealed that: the Engineering VPs for each BU had held a series of meetings to agree their expectations for the alliance; the Executive Steering Committee was now attended by representatives from the different business units who worked together to support the alliance; and the alliance managers had had a 'cordial' exchange with the Strategy VP around how they worked together. The alliance managers acknowledge that we had helped them understand the importance of mutual trust and understanding between the political stakeholders if the alliance was to function effectively.

THE EMOTIONAL PRESSURES OF WORKING WITH POWER AS AN INTERNAL

When I look back on our approach to the consulting project, I am much more aware of how political we had to be to take up our role. We worked within the existing power structures to establish our credibility and to influence those who were able to effect change. We were required to work very hard to move the project forward because we had not contracted at sufficiently senior levels at the start of the project. The senior level of the client group meant that we had few, if any, informal relationships within the client system, which meant we were not able to access what was going on 'behind the scenes'. Despite this, we were able to draw on our knowledge as insiders of how to get things done by working through the formal power structures in GC.

Throughout the project, I felt worried about saying what I thought to more senior figures, felt confused and overwhelmed by the complexity and enormity of the issues and noticed I often felt powerless. I also felt caught between the expectations of the CEO of the European BU and the cautiousness of the alliance managers. This reflected my participation in the tacit rules of the game and prevailing structures of power. At points in the project, our powerlessness manifested itself as apathy or a sense that we were the only ones who seemed to care about making changes. These emotional responses can be understood as representing the denied feelings of helplessness and confusion inside GC that were projected onto us.

Summary and Conclusion

This case highlights the complex, multi-level and messy power dynamics that are present in internal consulting projects in large systems. Power was present in almost every aspect of our work and in our relationships with the different people, groups and organizations in the system. Such dynamics need to be understood in terms of the strategic, economic and technical interdependencies between political actors in the client system. They also reflected implicit and largely unconscious assumptions around power on the part of the representatives of the different organizations. Our work addressed these issues by exploring, making explicit and re-negotiating how decisions were made and who participated in the process of decision-making. We were able to translate the underlying fears and anxieties of the alliance managers and BU leaders into legitimate concerns and interests that needed to be explored and negotiated in bounded forums and structures. The clarification of goals, tasks, roles and boundaries proved to be helpful in containing the anxieties of the senior leaders inside GC. This offered sufficient containment of anxiety to enable mature debate and decision making rather than the collapsing into informal political manoeuvring or competitive power dynamics.

Our work brought about a degree of change in the nature of the power relations that were enacted in relation to the alliance inside GC. This could be understood as a movement from a competitive power struggle to a form of power which is closer to Arendt's ideas of the capacity of different parties to act together to achieve something that they could not individually (Arendt 1958). The different business units started to re-negotiate how they worked together in the alliance to achieve their strategic interests. This represented a move towards a relational view of power and a shift from power as a zero-sum game. The case highlights how power relations are not simply organized hierarchically with power residing at the top of the organization. If anything, it highlights how, in this case, the assumption by the alliance managers that power resides at the top of the hierarchy worked against change. In our work with them, we helped them to gradually take up their role and exert influence with individuals above them in the hierarchy. It is also notable that they were exercising their power to exclude the Chairman and Strategy VP from the consulting process.

There are challenges and risks for the internal OD Consultant in taking up a position in the existing power structures when the task often involves work on power dynamics in organizations. This is a paradoxical position which can be experienced as an ongoing tension for the internal. When I finished the project, I became more aware of my own relatedness to the organization and how this had influenced my work. At times, I was seduced by my sense of status in being invited into the top echelons of the hierarchy. I also acted into my own omnipotent fantasies of being able to bring about change to a level and degree that is beyond the possible. Throughout much of the work, I struggled with feelings of powerlessness and a sense of being overwhelmed by the enormity of the task.

In concluding this chapter, I would like to return to Foucault's (1988) thinking on power. He encouraged a stance of understanding how power operates in specific contexts and to question that which is presented as definitive, untouchable, obvious, or immobile. Perhaps the central challenge for internals is to maintain a position on the edge of the client system where they both participate in the existing power dynamics while simultaneously revealing and questioning them. This can be a vulnerable position from which to operate and it requires a sensitivity to the 'rules of the game' and preparedness to claim one's authority.

References

Alderfer, C.P. 1980. The methodology of organizational diagnosis. *Professional Psychology*, 11(3), 459–68.

Bachrach, P. and Baratz, M.S. 1970. *Power and Poverty: Theory and Practice*. New York: Oxford University Press.

Bion, W.R. 1961. *Experiences in Groups*. London: Tavistock.

Clegg, S.R. 1975. *Power, Rule and Domination*. London: Routledge.

Crompton, R. 1993. *Class and Stratification: An Introduction to Current Debates*. Cambridge: Polity Press.

Dahl, R.A. 1957. The concept of power. *Behavioral Science*, 2 (3), 201–15.

Elias, N. 1978. *What is Sociology?* New York: Columbia State University.

Eriksen, T.H. 2001. *Small Places, Large Issues: An Introduction to Social and Cultural Anthropology.* 2nd Edition. London: Pluto Press.

Foucault, M. 1972. *The Archaeology of Knowledge and the Discourse on Language.* New York: Pantheon Books.

Foucault, M. 1980. *Power/Knowledge: Selected Interviews and Other Writings 1972– 1977.* London: Harvester.

Foucault, M. 1988. Power, moral values, and the intellectual. An interview with Michel Foucault by Michael Bess, *History of the Present*, 4, Spring, 11–13.

French, J.R.P. and Raven, B. 1968. The bases of social power, in *Group Dynamics: Research and Theory*, 3rd Edition, edited by D. Cartwright and A.F. Zander. New York: Harper and Row.

Giddens, A. 1984. *The Constitution of Society: Outline of the Theory of Structuration.* Cambridge: Polity Press.

Hayward, C.R. 1998. De-facing power. *Polity*, 31(1), 1–22.

Hindess, B. 1996. *Discourses of Power: From Hobbes to Foucault.* Oxford: Blackwell Publishers.

Hirschhorn, L. 1988. *The Workplace Within.* Cambridge, MA: MIT Press.

Holti, R. 2002. Engaging with client politics during entry and contracting. The Tavistock Institute's Advanced Organizational Consulting Program, 2002.

Kolb, D. and Frohman, A. 1970. An organizational development approach to consulting. *Sloan Management Review*, 12 (1), 51–65.

Lukes, S. 1974. *Power: A Radical View.* London: Macmillan.

Pfeffer, J. 1981. *Power in Organizations.* Cambridge: Ballinger Publishing Company.

Scott, B. 2008. Consulting on the inside, in *ASTD Handbook for Workplace Learning Professionals*, edited by E. Biech. Alexandria, VA: ASTD Press, 671–89.

Weber, M. 1978. *Economy and Society: An Outline of Interpretive Sociology.* Edited by G. Roth and C. Wittich. Berkeley, CA: University of California Press.

Winnicott, D. 1971. *Playing and Reality.* Middlesex: Penguin.

Wright, C. 2009. Inside out? Organizational membership, ambiguity and the ambivalent identity of the internal consultant. *British Journal of Management*, 20 (3), 309–22.

2

Strategic Moments in Internal Consulting: Introducing Functional Learning Environments in a Social Care Organization

Pauline Holland

In this chapter, I offer a reflective account of my experience of setting up and managing an internal consultancy service within a large UK voluntary sector organization during my tenure as Learning and Development Manager. I use the concept of functional/dysfunctional learning cycles (Vince and Martin 1993; Morrison 2005) to critique the establishment and on-going delivery of the consulting service. I describe elements of the internal consulting service that I believe went some way towards helping to build a more functional learning environment. I reflect on key 'strategic moments' (Vince 2004) that I encountered in the development and implementation of the service that suggests more dysfunctional learning cycles at play. Strategic moments are the moments when individuals and groups are confronted with making a choice to face and work through or to deny uncomfortable emotions arising from feelings of anxiety, doubts and uncertainties. I reflect on the significant challenge facing internal consultants as they seek to support individuals, groups and whole systems to build more functional learning environments and conclude on the supports necessary for consultants undertaking this challenging work.

Introduction

Over a period of six years, I set up and managed an internal consulting service within the Learning and Development function of a large voluntary sector (not-for-profit) organization. Prior to this, I worked in the youth justice field, working with and managing services for children and young people involved in offending behaviour – both within the public and voluntary sectors, including this same organization. Anyone familiar with this field will know that this work is personally very demanding. It requires a capacity for tolerating primitive anxieties stirred up in the worker in response to the client's issues and concerns, personal doubts about possibly doing more harm than good, as well as the ability to work with and continually assess risk. I made the transition from the frontline delivery and management of services to a learning and development role because I believed in the important contribution that a strong organizational learning culture could play in supporting frontline staff in undertaking this challenging work.

The organization had grown in size and complexity over the preceding 10- to 15-year period. Spans of control had expanded to accommodate the growth, and middle managers had become more outward facing in order to secure and sustain funding for the services in a competitive external environment. Supervision – a model that balanced providing support with accountability – was replaced for frontline managers with 'business meetings' where key result areas were identified and monitored. The emotional world of work appeared to have been subjugated in favour of goals and targets. These changes left some frontline managers and their teams feeling unsupported in their difficult and challenging task. As the new Learning and Development Manager, I was committed to addressing this need for more effective forms of support and containment.

Work Context

The voluntary sector, or third sector as it is also known, had experienced significant change over the preceding decade or more, precipitated by changes in government policy promoting greater involvement of the sector in public service delivery and policy development. This contributed to substantial growth and expansion of the sector. Consequently, organizations such as this grew in size and complexity. In return for this new work, governments required voluntary sector organizations to develop more 'business-like' practices and to engage with what was known as 'the modernizing agenda'. The impact of this agenda was to create a shift in culture and practice, creating tensions around the definition of the organization's primary task. Rice and Miller (1967) define the primary task of an organization as the task it must perform if it is to survive. In increasingly complex environments, there is seldom a single task that is necessary for survival and the issue of the primary task is often a contested one within organizations. During this period of growth the organization's primary task had evolved from an exclusive focus on delivering frontline services to vulnerable families to incorporate influencing activities, e.g., influencing public policy. While senior management, through strategic documents, sought to emphasize the equanimity or interdependence of service delivery and influencing activities, there was for some in the service delivery function a growing sense of the 'tail wagging the dog'.

The organization provided a range of services for vulnerable families. This work, while hugely rewarding, is also emotionally demanding and anxiety provoking. Expectations placed on organizations and professionals working in this arena by communities, politicians and wider society are often unrealistic and unhelpful, but they exist and must be managed in some way.

The emotional impact of working in human services is well documented in the Tavistock Clinic's edited book entitled *The Unconscious at Work* (Obholzer and Zagier Roberts 1994). In this work they use a psychoanalytic/psychodynamic frame of reference, normally associated with the one-to-one therapeutic relationship, to shed light on the complexities of working with vulnerable, damaged or damaging individuals and families. They highlight the various ways in which professionals and their institutions absorb primitive anxieties from the service users and how, in response, individuals and their institutions unconsciously develop defences against those anxieties. These defences invariably impede the individual's and the institution's capacity for undertaking this challenging work.

Menzies Lyth (1988) proposed 'that the success and viability of a social institution are intimately connected with the techniques it uses to contain anxiety' (78). The nature of the anxiety, she argues, is intimately connected to the primary task of the institution, which in this particular organization is concerned with alleviating human suffering. I envisaged the internal consulting model as one such technique for containing anxiety, thus helping to build a stronger emotional container for the work.

I envisaged that an internal consulting provision would contribute to the development of a more sustainable 'functional learning environment' in which practitioners and managers could openly acknowledge and work with anxieties, uncertainties and risks inherent in the work (Morrison 2005). I believed that the traditional training and development model that focused primarily on the individual's learning and development needs was no longer sufficient. Ordinarily a broad suite of training courses would be available for individuals to apply for and participate in according to identification of individual learning needs. The training courses were highly valued by the individuals and could be understood to be part of the reward system of the organization. It was not my intention to do away with the training courses per se. I was concerned, however, that in and of itself this approach had limited impact at the team and organizational levels. Individuals attending the training courses, particularly more in-depth practice focused programmes, were often left frustrated at their inability to help influence changes to practice at the level of the team. Vince (2004), in his work *Rethinking Strategic Learning*, writes about the collective work required by the group/team to successfully implement change. I wanted to shift the emphasis of the learning and development resource to support 'team learning' (Senge 1990) and in doing so build capacity for organizational learning. I therefore worked with others in my team to reposition the training department as an internal consulting service that could purposefully contribute to the creation of a learning culture that would enhance team and organizational learning. As I look back on this endeavour, I see that we enjoyed limited success.

Model of Internal Consulting – Functional Learning Environment

Morrison (2005), a leading UK specialist in social care policy and practice issues, advocated the value of creating functional learning environments which would better safeguard those using social care services while appropriately supporting the professionals involved in undertaking this demanding work. In the functional learning environment, the focus is on learning from experience. Briefly speaking, a functional learning cycle evolves directly from the individual's (and group's) capacity to tolerate anxiety, anxiety that arises in part from the experience of carrying out the work:

> *Anxiety is tolerated → uncertainty is acknowledged → individuals and groups can take appropriate risks/experiments → stay with the on-going struggle of not knowing → before reaching insight and/or achieving resolution.*

In contrast, in dysfunctional learning environments:

Anxiety is suppressed → individuals/groups retreat to fight/flight responses → this leads to defensiveness and avoidance → which, in turn, contributes to a shared denial → often resulting in disengagement with the challenge/task in hand and arrival at a place of 'willing ignorance'.
(Vince 2004)

Vince (2004) refers to the 'strategic moments' in which individuals and groups are faced with making a choice about confronting and working through or denying such anxieties. These choices appear to be made in an instant, informed in part by the established norms of the individual, group or whole system.

Morrison (2005) viewed the supervisory relationship – the relationship between the social care practitioner and their manager – as the cornerstone in creating a functional learning cycle. He developed a supervision framework around the functional learning model that was embraced by many social care organizations, including my own. I intended that the Internal Consulting service would further build on the supervisory relationship, enhancing team learning across the organization.

The internal consulting service consisted of four consultants, including me. Two of the consultants were located in the two regional offices (subsets of HQ) while the other consultant and I were based in the national head office (see Figure 2.1 below).

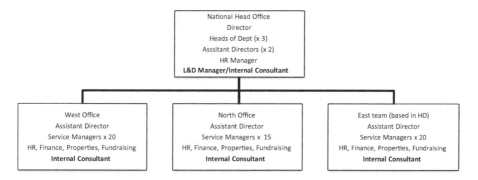

Figure 2.1   **Regional structure**

This was not the consultants' only remit. They continued to provide specialist training to operational staff and functional units across geographical boundaries. The experience of holding multiple roles with quite different, and often competing, demands frequently proved difficult to manage – at both an individual and collective level.

Identifying Issues and Starting Work

For the most part Assistant Directors and Service Managers requested help directly from the consultants. Initially, the most typical request was to help facilitate a teambuilding event. For some teams, teambuilding was a routine annual event. Increasingly, however, the request for consultancy support to teams arose out of the need for managers and teams to make sense of and respond to changes in their external environment, e.g., changes in funding arrangements required changes in service design.

The consultant followed a cycle of planned change model (Kolb and Frohman 1970) to structure their engagement with the manager and the team.

- Entry and contracting.

- Diagnosis.

- Data gathering and feedback.

- Implementation.

- Evaluation amd follow through.

This model supported the consultant in adopting a collaborative consulting style (Block 2000) emphasizing that the client in this work was the whole team. This was important in reassuring team members that the consultant was not simply brought in to help implement the manager's wishes. The consultant worked to secure agreement about how the diagnosis/discovery process would be undertaken and how the feedback would be shared, and then worked with the team to jointly plan the intervention.

Some examples of consultancy provided included:

- Work with a large service team to help the team address the impact of externally-driven changes affecting the way they provided the service, contributing to the design and development of a change management plan.

- Intervention with a service team dealing with concerning levels of sickness absence, using an agreed diagnostic tool to collate feedback from individual team members to surface and work through issues and concerns and jointly develop mechanisms to address issues of stress in the workplace.

- Service redesign in response to demands from funding providers.

- Consultancy to Operational Management Team on identifying workable criteria for prioritizing allocation of voluntary funds.

- Action learning facilitation for service managers.

Key Challenges in Embedding the Model/Service

I want now to consider three strategic moments that I encountered during the lifetime of the service in which, on reflection, I avoided facing and working through uncomfortable emotions in myself – and others – choosing instead to work from a place of willing ignorance (Vince 2004). There were, of course, many more such moments throughout this assignment. However, I'm highlighting these particular instances because of their significance in relation to my overall aim to build a more functional learning environment. I think they are illustrative of the challenge one faces as an internal change agent endeavouring to bring about sustainable changes in organizational learning.

The first moment concerns my efforts to secure backing for the internal consulting service from my senior management team colleagues; the second such moment occurred at the mid-stage review of the service; while the third moment relates to my attempt to take up an internal consulting role to the Director who was leading a potential organizational redesign change project.

SEEKING BACKING FOR MY PROPOSAL

The first such strategic moment came at the very beginning of the development of the service. I tested my initial proposal to shift the focus of the L&D remit from one of training delivery to that of providing internal consultancy through talking with the Director (my line manager) and by sounding out a few of my peers. I then presented a formal proposal paper to my colleagues on the senior management team. The standard practice on these occasions was for the Director to ask the colleague responsible for the proposal paper to take the group through the paper one page at a time to clarify any points or answer any questions and then the Director would invite each member of the team to say whether they backed the proposal or not. From memory two colleagues from a group of about ten managers raised some questions about the proposal, primarily about what the proposed changes would mean in terms of existing training provision. Each group member, when invited to declare their position by the Director, indicated their backing for the proposal and I appeared to be given the green light by the group to proceed with my initiative. There was a small caveat based on the questions raised by my two colleagues. The Director highlighted that while I had the backing of the senior management team, I still had my work cut out to get the backing of the service managers whom he thought would need reassurance that this change wouldn't affect the training provision that staff were used to. This was my first experience of presenting a proposal paper to my colleagues. I felt relieved and excited – a little triumphant even – to get the go ahead for my initiative. As I stand back now to reflect on and make sense of my experience of leading and managing the internal consultancy service I am more curious to understand what was really happening in the group around this key decision-making moment.

The notion of organizations as 'political systems' (Morgan 1986) provides me with a helpful frame for analyzing and thinking about what might have been going on during this initial stage. I recognize that I adopted a selling approach when developing and presenting my proposal: I acted politically within the system. Prior to presenting the paper at the meeting, I used my influence with the Director and a few other key players to develop allies that I could rely on to support my proposal. I used my proposal paper to highlight deficiencies in the current provision and sold the benefits that the new model could be expected to deliver, including greater levels of support to frontline staff and their managers – a key concern for a number of the operational managers within the management group. During the Q&A session I sought to provide reassurance to those colleagues raising questions about current training provision levels by indicating that the level of provision would remain constant – the only change being that instead of L&D staff delivering the training we could expect to directly involve those staff in the services who had the relevant expertise and who were eager to develop in this way. It seems to me that the selling approach adopted by me and that I believe was representative of prevailing organizational dynamics at the time, reflected a fight/flight choice in me – and the group as a whole – to avoid confronting and exploring the implications of the intended change in the nature of organizational learning that I was proposing. The data for this hypothesis, I believe, lies in part in what I did not say in my proposal paper. I did not make all of my thinking and reasoning explicit about why I was proposing this model. I did not, for example, include the data that I held as a relatively recent service manager concerning the power relations and perceived power inequalities between Senior Management Team (SMT) and service managers, including for example, that a significant number of service managers felt unsupported, disenfranchised and excluded from key decision making processes in the organization. Had I found a way to speak to this in my paper and in discussion with my colleagues, it may have served to surface concerns amongst SMT members that the proposed change to the role of the L&D consultant could result in the politics of the organization being put up for examination, particularly concerning how and where decisions were made. The fact that I didn't approach the paper in this way is perhaps best explained by my colleague Andrew Day's observations in his chapter on 'Power and the Internal: Working on the Edge' (Chapter 1). He says of internal practitioners, 'They can become so attuned to the power dynamics in their organizations that they are unaware of how they participate in them'. It never occurred to me at the time to approach the task in any other way.

MID STAGE REVIEW – HANDLING CLIENT FEEDBACK

The second strategic moment presented itself at the mid-stage point of the life cycle of the consultancy provision. Just over three years into delivering the internal consulting service, I arranged for an external consultant to undertake a client feedback survey in preparation for a two-day retreat for the Internal Consulting staff group. The survey sampled managers representing the different client groups and different levels of seniority within the organization. In addition, each consultant was interviewed to gather additional data.

The feedback presented a largely positive picture of the perceived value of the internal consulting service, particularly at the service delivery level of the organization. In many situations where internal consultancy was provided, managers and their teams valued the relationship they established with the consultants and the learning they achieved. One manager noted that, as a result of the consultant's involvement, the 'team gained knowledge of and understanding of the [emotional] impact of the work on the workers'. Another commented that the consultant provided a 'holding environment to let hard issues be looked at and addressed' while another reflected that the intervention by the consultant 'moved a lot of stuck-ness [in the team]'. General sentiment about the perceived value of the consultancy intervention amongst its supporters is captured in one manager's comments: 'Consultants have a different view that is very effective as a counter to a lot of the hurried, crisis-driven decisions that are often taken'.

The feedback suggested that, in their work with teams, consultants supported and encouraged functional learning cycle behaviours, namely behaviours that enabled different voices and perspectives to be heard, doubts and anxieties to be explored and worked through, supporting teams to achieve insight and reach shared conclusions about the best way forward. Anxieties associated with changes in the external environment, combined with the profound anxieties related to the work that had to be managed, at times threatened to implode within teams, reducing the group's capacity to think together and engage in creative problem solving. Having a consultant present appeared to help provide a kind of safe container for the anxieties of individuals and groups, enabling group members to speak out and to hear one another. Much of the feedback from our clients indicated that it was often only after such interventions had taken place that it was possible for the team to engage in collective problem solving.

A few key issues for consideration emerged in the data gathering exercise. The feedback indicated some general confusion about the role of the consultants – what they did or did not do now – and a perception about the lack of a process for prioritizing the competing demands placed upon the consultants. Some managers expressed concern about an apparent reduction in training and voiced dissatisfaction with the loss of control over their L&D budget – the move to a centralized L&D budget, held by me and my department, had come about after the launch of the internal consultancy service and had been determined at the highest level of the organization. Perhaps one of the most significant comments to come out of the feedback survey was expressed by one of the senior managers who voiced a concern about the impact on the consultants of listening to staff concerns, which the manager referred to as 'soaking up a lot of the organization's mess'. This apparent concern for the wellbeing of the consultants could also be understood as a concern for or an expression of guilt feelings about senior management's 'failure' to provide adequate support and containment for the work – which in itself would be a kind of mirroring of the client system issues. If thought about as a below the surface comment (Huffington et al. 2004), the notion of organizational mess might be a reference to the dangers associated with emotions 'spilling out' and perhaps a desire or a wish to 'keep a lid' on things.

On reflection, although I recognized these as key issues at the time, I failed to use the data feedback as an opportunity to dialogue with managers via appropriate forums across the organization about such matters as role clarity, expectations and goal agreement. In addition, it would have been helpful to use such exchanges as an opportunity for the internal consultants to share some of the organizational themes that emerged during their work with teams. An opportunity for dialogue and reflection with managers on the feedback may have allowed for joint consideration of mechanisms for providing containment to frontline service staff, including appropriate mechanisms for meaningful engagement of all staff, particularly frontline managers, on key organizational issues. So why did it not occur to me share and explore the feedback with the wider client system? At the time, there was strong pressure on the Director to relinquish direct line management of the L&D function and to have it subsumed under HR. I felt I was fighting a rear-guard action to prevent that from happening. Questions about where OD/Internal Consulting should sit within an organization are common. I was of the view that we needed to remain independent of HR. In part I assume that it felt too risky to raise my head above the parapet at that point. I resolved to keep going with what was working well, increase my team's efforts to communicate what we did and improve the recording of our work in order that we could better evidence our value add – a 'try harder' kind of response. I can now see, however, that my choice was also a kind of fight/flight response, an instinctive desire to avoid opening up a discussion about the resource at a time of increasing uncertainty about the role and positioning of L&D in the broader organizational arena. I wonder if, however, by avoiding the opportunity for dialogue with managers on the feedback, I inadvertently contributed to a general weakening of organizational support for this L&D resource at a time when it was most necessary to engender active support.

ROLE CONFLICT, ROLE AMBIGUITY – CHALLENGES FOR INTERNAL CONSULTANTS AND CHANGE AGENTS

The third 'strategic moment' that I want to consider occurred towards the end of my tenure as L&D Manager. The Director initiated a review of the organization's design, primarily the organization's structure. I recall that this review was intended by the Director to respond to a number of issues related to continued growth in the organization. The issues were: a recognition that frontline managers and their teams had felt increasingly distanced from decision-making processes as spans of control had expanded; frontline services required increased support to deal with the consequences of growth; and the Director and others felt that there was an increasingly urgent need to adapt our structure to ensure the agency remained well placed to respond to opportunities in an increasingly competitive external environment.

The Director sought my help and support with some aspects of this change initiative: help in thinking about the design for a meeting of the corporate strategic decision making group – the group identified by the Director to lead on the redesign project (and a group that I was also a member of) – and help in planning and facilitating the consultation event with the wider management group. We also had regular conversations about responses to the emerging proposals. However, we never explicitly discussed my role. All the discussions we had about the change initiative were informal and took place within the context of the line manager-direct report relationship. This lack of explicit agreement about roles, not surprisingly, created some difficulties in our working relationship as the change project got underway. Due to wider organizational influences, the organizational redesign initiative was halted, and I was left to try to make sense of what had happened between the Director and me and to consider what my experience might tell me about taking up an internal consulting role with one's manager as the primary client.

In my view, the point at which the Director, acting as change agent for this initiative, asked for my help was a 'strategic moment'. I could have explored what kind of help the Director was looking for from me and perhaps even negotiated a more explicit role for myself in the change process. Instead, I assumed an invitation to work collaboratively with the Director, to bring my knowledge on organizational design and my expertise on group processes to bear on the project and to be an active agent in the process alongside the Director. As I look back, I believe that the Director expected me to take up a more passive role in advising and supporting the Director as change agent, to act, as it were, as a 'pair of hands' (Block 2000). I felt frustrated. I became increasingly uncomfortable and actively resisted this role. Two issues were at stake for me. Firstly, throughout my tenure as L&D Manager, I worked openly to try to engineer a shift towards more democratic processes for influencing and decision-making within the organization. This particular organizational change initiative provided a significant opportunity to increase the involvement of all managers in key organizational decision-making processes. It was my assumption that this was an explicit intention of the redesign project. I was keen, therefore, to ensure it was manifest in the consultation and redesign process. Secondly, I wanted to carve out a change consultation role for myself (and eventually my team) at a more strategic level in the organization. Up until that point I felt that our consulting role was being restricted to an operational level, impeding opportunities for organizational learning. As I have reflected on this experience, I see that I adopted a somewhat covert political role in the system, using whatever influence and power I felt I had to try get the Director (and other senior management colleagues) to acknowledge and work with the voice of frontline managers. This was a very risky and, some might say, an unwise strategy. Block's (2000) suggestion, that some managers who have a preference for the consultant to act as a pair of hands may experience attempts by the consultant to work more collaboratively as an act of insubordination, seems apt. This has got to be a very real concern for individuals and teams taking up internal consulting roles in institutions when consulting to colleagues more senior in the organization, whether line manager or not.

Some Reflections

I've drawn out these particular three occasions because I think they are illustrative of the challenge for any internal change agent working to build more functional learning cycles. As I reflect on these three strategic moments I can now see how, at times, I found it difficult to navigate skillfully the multiple roles that I occupied, namely, my functional, organizational and professional roles. This blurring of roles was, I think, fuelled by the political nature of the organization that I was inculcated into by dint of having worked in it for several years before taking up my new role as L&D Manager. The need to understand the political machinations of organizational life and to consider how they both contribute to and inhibit organizational learning is a key challenge for internal change agents and consultants.

As I reflect on the experience overall, I can see that the consultancy team did successfully contribute to the occurrence of more functional learning cycles at a team level. I believe the internal consultants' role provided a helpful containing mechanism for managers and their teams as they faced their own strategic moments in their work. Through the consultants' interventions, many managers and their teams found ways to slow down and work through important issues and concerns, enabling them to find their own creative solutions to what often initially felt like intractable problems. In this work, the consultants contributed to the health of the institution.

It was only possible, however, to consult so far into the system. It was in reality much more difficult to replicate the approach that encouraged more functional learning cycles at a strategic level in the organization. Why was this? Drawing on the data from my own 'strategic moments', I would hypothesize that these moments reflected a deeper, more hidden need in the organization to avoid conflict, to avoid hearing and working with dissenting voices for fear of a sort of collective unraveling. Perhaps part of the consultant's role was indeed to soak up the organizational mess as expressed as a concern by one of the senior managers. It seems that this organizational mess needed to be kept separate from the business of strategy development. Questions concerning the strategic direction of the organization, namely, the commitment to simultaneously achieve growth in service delivery *and* exert political influence on policy development externally appeared to be kept separate from operational matters and thereby outside the jurisdiction of organizational learning.

A Final Thought – Support for the Internal Consultant

Internal consultants do inevitably absorb aspects of the organization's (emotional) 'mess'. Their capacity to do so in a way that is thoughtful and containing for the client is their 'value-add'. However, if the consultants are not able, over time, to speak to the issues and organizational themes arising from their interventions with managers and teams, there is a real danger that they are left holding intense and painful emotions that they won't know what to do with. They risk getting caught up in the emotional undertow of the organization and becoming identified with the dissociative aspects of the emotional life of the organization. It's important to be able to consider what supports internal consultants require if they are to remain intact and able to contribute to the health of an organization. Interventions that support individual consultants and consultancy teams to develop their capacity to recognize 'strategic moments' both for themselves as well their clients are essential. Some form of shadow consultancy support could prove vital. A shadow consultant, an experienced consultant who is outside the client system, works with the internal consultant to help them think about what is going on inside the system and attends to what needs to shift inside the internal consultant to enable them to be more effective in taking up their role inside their organization (Hawkins and Smith 2006). This would help the internal consultant to be mindful of the different roles they occupy and to think carefully about how to navigate the organization's political terrain in ways that encourage healthy and functional learning cycle behaviours.

References

Block, P. 2000. *Flawless Consulting: A Guide To Getting Your Expertise Used*. 2nd Edition. New York: Jossey-Bass/Pfeiffer.

Hawkins, P. and Smith, N. 2006. *Coaching, Mentoring and Organizational Consultancy: Supervision and Development*. Berkshire and New York: Open University Press.

Huffington, C., Armstrong, D., Halton, W., Hoyle, L. and Pooley, J. 2004. *Working Below the Surface: The Emotional Life of Contemporary Organizations*. Tavistock Clinic Series. London: Karnac Books.

Kolb, D. and Frohman, A. 1970. An organizational development approach to consulting. *Sloan Management Review*, 12(1), 51–65.

Menzies, I.L. 1988. *Containing Anxiety in Institutions: Selected Essays*. Vol. 1. London: Free Association Books.

Morgan, G. 1986. *Images of Organization*. Thousand Oaks, CA: SAGE.

Morrison, T. 2005. *Staff Supervision in Social Care: Making a Real Difference for Staff and Service Users*. Brighton: Pavilion.

Obholzer, A. and Zagier Roberts, V. 1994. *The Unconscious at Work: Individual and Organizational Stress in the Human Service*. London and New York: Routledge.

Rice, E.J. and Miller, A.K. 1967. *Systems of Organisation: The Control of Task and Sentience Boundaries*. London: Tavistock Publications Ltd.

Senge, P. 1990. *The Fifth Discipline: The Art & Practice of the Learning Organization*. London, Sydney, Auckland and Parktown: Century Business.

Vince, R. and Martin, L. 1993. Inside action learning: An exploration of the psychology and politics of the action learning model. *Management Education and Development*, 24(3), 205–21.

Vince, R. 2004. *Rethinking Strategic Learning in Routledge Studies in Human Resource Development*. London: Routledge.

3

Dining with the Devil

Lord Victor O. Adebowale CBE

Community Therapy (CT) is a UK charity established in 1964 to provide psychological therapies to people with drug, alcohol and mental health challenges. Many of its clients had been former members of the armed forces but were now members of the general public. Access to the service was through referral by family doctors, local social services departments and National Health Service (NHS) hospitals. In the 1980s, CT had branched out into the delivery of services to people with learning disabilities, having been asked to take over the running of an old NHS-provided service for people with mild to moderate learning disabilities. This proved a success in that other NHS providers of disability provision approached CT to take over their services as well. CT had also successfully competed to win a number of contracts to do with the closure of old learning disability service provision. These involved moving people with learning disabilities, and sometimes mental health challenges, from NHS institutions into community and independent living services.

CT's main income was obtained through fundraising and the organization had enjoyed a high-profile royal patron until the early 1990s when this patron, having decided to reduce commitments, withdrew their patronage. In 1995, CT's income was approximately 80 per cent fundraised income, however it was becoming increasingly difficult to raise income in this way. The expense of adopting the latest fundraising techniques was proving difficult due to increased competition for both trust funds and high value donor contributions. Other charities were seen to have more 'attractive causes' and some donors had expressed a reluctance to give to a charity that worked with drug users. While the educative process of engaging funders in CT's work sometimes led to funds being donated, it was proving both time consuming and expensive to engage the main donors in lengthy discussions. Paying for an expert and expensive fundraising team that may or may not result in donations wasn't working. By the end of the 1990s, the ratio of spending on fundraising to the income obtained was moving from a positive ratio to negative one. A number of corporate donors had taken the decision to stop funding both CT's drug and alcohol service and had pulled out of funding CT's other activities. CT had grown a profusion of services through its good fundraising and service expansion years and was now providing services across the country but was facing shrinking fundraising incomes and growing service provision costs.

CT's board of governors consisted of 20 people, many with backgrounds in local government, health, trade union administration, fundraising and voluntary sector governance. Tensions had started to appear among the board members relating to the growth of CT from a small London-based charity to a significant provider of substance misuse services, to a provider of substance misuse services, mental health and learning disability services across four locations in England. CT was now employing 500 people and had developed the necessary infrastructure to deliver services legally and safely.

Between the years 1990 and 2001 CT had been led by four different chief executive officers (CEO) appointed by the board to stabilize the organization's finances and structure. The board identified that there was a need to cut costs across CT, while increasing fundraising income and grants, particularly from local government where a significant amount of CT's work was now engaged. Each CEO had made some progress against this agenda but tensions between the centre and the staff in the services provided by CT were increasing and were cited in the reasons given for the departure of each of the CEOs during this period.

In 2001 the situation at CT had come near to crisis as the departure of the last CEO had left a gap that was filled by the chair until a new appointment could be made. My entry into CT was as a result of the process to recruit the fifth CEO. During the recruitment process, a number of senior staff who were responsible for regional service management were approached by the chair of the board with the idea that CT could be run by a collective of senior managers. The idea was that each of CT's services would become autonomous with its own local board and operate as a franchise model. Thus, there would be no requirement to appoint an expensive CEO at the centre. The board response was to continue the appointment process for the new CEO. I applied for the post and obtained it starting my tenure in late 2001.

My background in charitable administration was as CEO of a high-profile charity that had relied on fundraised income and which had increased its nonfundraised income over a five-year period. My application for the role of CEO of CT had stressed my experience as a charity CEO and my ability to raise funds. My career up until that point had also been very much about entering organizations that were in financial difficulties but were also facing internal challenges such as a lack of clarity of roles, confusing and unresolved debates about strategic direction and often difficult governance situations. In my experience, board members are often in tense debate with each other as to the purpose of the board and its relationship with the appointed executive. While this had been my personal career history, at that point I had not undertaken any formal training in management (I later was able to contextualize my career experiences through training and obtaining the MA in Advanced Organizational Consultation at the Tavistock and City University). Upon entering CT as its new CEO I was conscious of: (1) the many debates about the need for a new CEO and (2) the feeling (sometimes expressed forcefully) that like previous CEOs I would not be around for very long, just 'long enough to get my next job'.

Crossing the Threshold

My formal entry into CT was at a board meeting that took place on September 11, 2001. During the meeting, news came through of the twin towers atrocity in New York and the chair suspended the meeting so that the board could see the news before returning to the agenda and the item entitled 'Introduction of CT's new CEO'. This agenda item began with a board member asking me to set out the challenges for CT as I saw them. This was very much the first point of contact with the board as organizational client to my consultancy and the start of an attempt to begin a process of engagement with the board to address a number of challenges. The first of these was the financial situation, which was deteriorating, with fundraising effectively failing to meet its own costs. Local councils, as contractors for CT services, were refusing to increase grant income to cover the costs of ensuring CT had an infrastructure capable of managing the range of client needs (substance misuse, mental health and services to people with learning disabilities all of whom would be deemed as vulnerable). The second area of challenge was the internal culture. This was charitable in the sense that money was a problem for those at the centre (whose job it was to raise money through fundraising) while frontline staff did the work of actual service provision and had no concern with issues of financial viability. The final challenge was the idea of the federal franchised CT, which was live as an alternative to the current board and organizational structure. This had taken hold to the point where some CT services had started to ignore

CT management requests and were talking about establishing their own organization and developing relationships with local funders. In setting out these challenges I invited the board to engage with this analysis and in doing so acknowledged that should the board disagree with my analysis (which had been obtained by chatting with the CT's staff informally, prior to my arrival as CEO at my first board meeting), I would be in trouble. This would mean that my scouting (Kolb and Frohman 1970) had not built a platform for building a relationship with the board that would allow me to work with them on a joint plan to resolve the above challenges. In effect, my tenure as CEO and internal consultant would probably be short-lived.

The CT board had made a series of decisions to freeze posts across CT and previous CEOs had made both frozen and unfrozen posts a means of getting control over the financial situation. The board's actions had been mainly driven by the immediate approval or disapproval of expenditure. The experience reported to me during my entry into CT was one of being 'attached to a swinging pendulum' that seemed to lurch from one extreme to another.

CT's board (luckily for me) were happy to receive my analysis, which had the effect of moving the discussion from the immediate and tactical to the strategic and medium- to long-term. The time period that we had to resolve these matters was decreasing and yet there was a sense that shifting internal perceptions about what sort of organization CT actually was might help shift the other challenges the organization was facing from critical or a sense of crisis to a sense that they could be managed over time.

Crossing the threshold from outsider to insider in my relationship with CT occurred at the above meeting and from this point on I was on the inside as defined by the board appointees. In my first discussions with the chair of the board, it transpired that previous CEOs of CT had not stayed long because they had failed to engage the board in a view of the organization that was 'even slightly' beyond the need to freeze posts or unfreeze posts. They left because 'we didn't support their analysis of our problems because they had never presented us with one'.

Starting Work: Covert and Explicit

CT's executives and the rest of the organization saw the role of CEO and the board as outside and had not formerly been part of the debate about the future of the organization and whether the idea of the franchise CT was viable or not. This lack of involvement had resulted in two strategies being developed – one by the board as the strategy aimed at resolving the immediate challenge of the finances and another strategy that was being enacted by CT's staff, in spite of the board and executive, with variable support from members of the senior managers responsible for CT regional services.

At the time I did not see my role as CEO in consulting terms. Hindsight and education has since allowed my role at that time to be usefully structured as internal consultant to CT but in a way that could be described as covert (Gill and Johnson 1991) as opposed to explicit consulting. This involved a process of relationship building, interventions, action, evaluation and exit (as described by Kolb and Frohman in their work on consulting practice). Certainly my intent to keep my job and to help CT resolve its many challenges was not expressed loudly either to the executive or the board at that time for fear of withdrawal of the board's support. This would leave me in the position of the previous CEOs of the organization – completely outside.

The first decision I made was to continue with current frozen posts in order to steady the 'swinging pendulum' until we had agreed an appropriate organizational structure. The process of considering structure would also allow the issue of the franchising of CT to be aired fully so that the viability of such a plan might be examined. A series of round table discussions took place, firstly with members of the frontline service staff, then with area managers, followed by mixed groups of area managers and service staff so that we could explore the reality of a franchise model. Finally discussions took place with the executive and senior managers. These discussions reported back the outcomes of previous discussions so executives could take into account the views of frontline and senior managers as well as looking critically at the ideas presented. My thinking was that my participation in all these discussions was essential, both in establishing my entry into the executive and staff groups in CT and as a means of shifting perceptions that might lead to a shared endeavour resolving the challenges facing CT in the short-, medium- and long-term.

During the course of these discussions the issue of CT as a franchised, federated structure was discussed and the reality of franchised organizations was clarified. There was some confusion between the idea of franchise and the desire for CT services to be free of the centre, i.e., the board and the executive. The idea of a franchise was appealing because it provided the idea of freedom and stability and the possibility that individual services might escape the uncertainty associated with CT's future. During the discussion the introduction of some facts about how franchise operations actually run made the franchise idea less appealing. The first of these facts was that organizations that ran as franchises were actually more likely to be controlled by a very strict adherence to central bureaucracy than anything that CT services were used to, and this was particularly so in high risk areas of personal services, like the provision of addiction, mental health and services to people with learning disabilities. The other fact was that the majority of CT's services were simply not viable as individually franchised entities. How would they provide the necessary infrastructure to deliver a safe service in their localities unless they could negotiate increased grants from local councils and fundraise themselves – both of which were proving challenging for CT and would prove more so for individual CT services?

These discussions also revealed a deep confusion about the role of fundraising and CT as a 'charity bureaucracy' as it was referred to by some frontline service managers. Our charitable fundraising stance actually allowed the local councils and NHS institutions with whom CT did business to see CT as a cheap option. They could provide grants for services that were subsidised by CT fundraising efforts. The process of the discussion rounds (as they became known) shifted perceptions that the Executive of CT only gave instruction about as opposed to leading strategic debates about CT's current or future challenges. The sense of us-and-them, often referred to during these discussions, gradually became a joint effort to resolve the CT's challenges. This was helped by members of the organization knowing where phrases used by the executive to describe the organization's position came from. An example of this was the use of the term 'business' which was first used by a service manager who in frustration pointed out that CT 'was a business really and we need to stop pretending we were just a charity'. My role became translating the outputs of these discussions into a new strategy for CT that could be applied to the immediate challenge, as well as providing a platform for the long-term viability of the organization.

Consulting to Strategic Debates

The core of this strategy was to challenge the idea that CT as a charity could not be a business and to raise the idea that as a business we needed to take an objective view of our financial position. The idea of CT as a business was not something CT's board was comfortable with. The CT charity fundraising model, being seen as unsustainable by both the staff and the executive, created choices for individual board members, some of whom chose to leave. This reduced the number and type of board members that remained and enabled them to consider the challenge of running a charitable business as opposed to 'just a charity'.

CT's financial challenge lay in the view that as a charity we had to fundraise for services and should be grateful to receive grants (as opposed to contracts) for the remaining costs of the service. The problem with this model was all too apparent in that grants did not cover the full costs of providing the service and fundraising was accruing further costs. The shift to CT as a business enabled an approach to both local government and the NHS based on another term that came out of the discussion rounds – the idea of full cost recovery. This meant that we could establish the basis on which we charged for the services CT provides for service users through contracts with, not grants from, local government and the NHS. CT's service managers, executive and board had to accept that this may mean proactively closing services that were no longer viable financially and returning clients to other care. However the debate exposed what the alternative might be if we failed to negotiate new terms: unplanned closure of services due to uncontrolled loss of income.

This new strategy involved training senior managers in negotiating techniques and introducing a framework for understanding the costs of each service and what it would take to construct a contract for services as opposed to asking for a grant. The idea of finance being unconnected to the provision of care was challenged. During this period the term 'charity thinking' came into use to describe a way of thinking about care which did not involve thinking about the real costs of care and the impact on CT as a business. The fear was that such negotiations would result in the previous experience of rejection. However, the experience was that both local government and NHS institutions were willing to negotiate contracts because a contract with CT was cheaper than the alternative of closure and or private or even other charity providers. CT continued to bid for contracts and increased the rate of winning. The purpose of fundraising was increasingly called into question because of the diminishing returns for the cost and in 2002 the fundraising function was shut, thus establishing CT as a non-profit business (but still registered with the charity commission as a charity).

My role as CEO and in hindsight internal consultant had been established with the board as clients. My entry into the organization had been through the discussion rounds; these established me in my role as CEO and as internal consultant to the system (although without any formal contracting process). The expectation that I, like the other CEOs, would be departing after a year or so had dissolved through the experience of engaging through discussion, which had also changed perceptions about CT.

In 2003 CT was approached by Services in Public (SIB), a private sector company with a turnover of four billion pounds sterling. SIB was a major provider of a range of public services across local government, health and the prison services. The government of the day had initiated a programme of new prison building and was inviting tenders from providers of prison services to bid to both build and run prisons. SIB approached me as CEO of CT because of an article I had written on CT's approach to the provision of addiction and mental health service as a combined intervention to prisoners. CT's own services in prisons were facing significant challenges. Even though we could prove successful outcomes for individuals in prison, the prison service was proving difficult to work with and the cost of working with individual prison governors was prohibitive. CT had not engaged with any private sector organization in the past other than as a donor. The size of SIB would require a discussion about whether CT should be seen to be forming any partnership with SIB alongside the on-going work of accepting the commercial realities of being a non-profit business.

However, the alternative to sitting at the table with SIB was the possible closure of our service to the criminal justice system and the loss of a useful and proven model. The approach by SIB was reported to the board. In essence, their idea was that CT would provide psychosocial interventions alongside SIB's management of prisons. This was not dissimilar to the approach we were making already, albeit unsuccessfully, within the prison service. The prisons managed by SIB would be new prisons, won in the bids for the new contracts to be led by the government. In discussing the approach with members of the senior team at CT it became apparent that there were misgivings about whether we should enter in any kind of partnership with SIB or indeed any other type of for profit organization. As one manager put it, 'Victor expects us to dine with the devil'. As CEO of CT I had effectively entered the system and, as I have already described, crossed two boundaries:

1.   the board (as my client); and

2.   the organization, through engaging with the staff and executive.

Now, in a very real sense I found myself outside the organization (CT). The issue for me was not whether we engaged with SIB but whether CT could remain detached from some of the realities of delivering services to the public.

CT had successfully negotiated its relationships with local government and the NHS through changing its perception of itself from 'charity' to business (we had by then engaged in calling ourselves a social enterprise) and had in effect already dined with some of its devils. Could we remain true to our mission while developing relationships with those outside our perception of the kind of business CT had become? A summary of changes might look like the table below.

Table 3.1   Key CT characteristics before and after change effort

Before Change From the Inside	After Change From the Inside
Dependent on grants.	Contracts based on full cost recovery.
Fundraising fiasco.	Income generated through winning contracts.
No internal discussions with staff.	Internal dialogues.
No external discussions with client organizations.	Strategic debate.
No strategic debates.	Proactive culture with choices to discuss.
No choice – passive culture?	A clear business model/s.
No business model.	A business not a charity as the organization in the
Organization in the mind? = charity.	mind.

Working with People Like Us, Not Like Them

A number of meetings to discuss the approach with SIB were held. The first of these was with the CT board who were happy to go ahead and to my surprise saw the event as part of the new CT approach to business. However this was not reflected in meetings with the executive and senior managers who held strong views about partnership with SIB or anyone like them. Over a series of three meetings, I established that my role was to resolve whether we, and how we, would engage in *any* partnerships with *any* non-social enterprise body, rather than whether or not we should work with SIB.

This was enough of a brief to engage the executive and senior team. A series of dialogues was arranged with SIB. These events were designed collaboratively with executive and senior managers from CT as myth busters. I asked the question 'what do we know about SIB?' I also asked SIB to come to the event with the same set of questions. The meetings were arranged not to discuss the approach by SIB but to try and understand what and who they are as an organization. These discussions revolved around values and challenges and assumptions and took place over a period of three weeks and two daylong events. It emerged that CT could express a set of values and that these values were not that dissimilar to those expressed by managers and executives in SIB. Ideas held by both executive and management teams about how the 'other' worked also arose, and CT managers were able to draw on their experience of shifting relations with local government and the NHS to shift the perception of SIB managers. Their view was that CT people were not commercial and that doing business with CT was somehow a 'charitable' activity.

CT's senior managers asked the executive and the board whether they could go ahead with forming a partnership with SIB to deliver psychosocial interventions in SIB prison settings. As a result of this discussion it became easier for CT to enter into a number of such partnerships with commercial organizations not dissimilar to the partnership with SIB. The focus of my internal consulting role was entirely focused on CT; however, it is true to say that engagement with CT shifted SIB's perception of what kind of organization they could be. At the time of writing SIB are engaged in a review of their relationship with not-for-profit organizations.

The Role of CEO as Internal Consultant

In reflecting on the role of CEO as internal consultant and on the above experience, I now have the hindsight provided by both experience and learning. In summary, I can see that I used my role as CEO to negotiate consulting interventions with the board of CT, the executive and senior managers and the frontline workers within the business and also an external business-to-business collaboration with SIB.

The use of internal debates to elicit understanding was a matter of attempting to use the confusion and disconnects within CT as potential rather than something to avoid or apply answers to. The task was to help the people in my organization to gain confidence in their own ability to arrive at an appropriate perception of what CT was as an organization and why. To some extent the CEO role separates an individual from the organization, and this separation can be used to enter the organization from different angles. However each entry has to be negotiated by the guardians of that route. For example, my entry into CT initially was through the governance structure, the board, and had to be negotiated through contracting with the board. The same contract could not be used in entering the organization through the senior management team and executive in working through the SIB approach. In a sense, authorization of the role of CEO in this context comes from active engagement. The point is to contract with them as a consultant although this does not have to be a stated aim. I found it has worked to ensure that both authorization and credibility are not simply demanded but negotiated in the first instance and freely given in the second. I have asked the question, 'Could an external consultant have been used to achieve the same result?' The answer is probably no because the following would have been true: an external consultant would not have been able to negotiate an entry into the organization and would not have been given full authority by the board. The CEO role would continue to be questioned and would have been seen as incapable of leading change, and an external consultant would have enhanced the feeling that CT was being done to as opposed to done with.

This case describes an experience that required some challenging analysis as to my own role as CEO when faced with a situation that challenged the very purpose of the CEO role in an organization that was in a state of some internal conflict and external threats. At the time I was not as conscious as I am now as to the role of consulting practice in providing context and a theoretical basis for thinking about change interventions. However, the experience of my entry into CT encouraged me to take up and complete an MA in advanced organizational consulting with the Tavistock and City University. This has allowed me to do two things, firstly make sense of the above case in a way that I hope is helpful to others and secondly remain engaged with the idea of the permanent internal consultant within the current CT organization, with the officer role becoming less important than my role as a member of the board and senior leadership team.

References

Gill, J. and Johnson, P. 1991. *Research Methods for Managers*. London: Paul Chapman Publishing.

Kolb, D.A. and Frohman, A.L. 1970. An organization development approach to consulting. *Sloan Management Review*, 12(1), 51–65.

4

Managing Projects: How an Organization Design Approach Can Help

Robin C. Stevens and Susan Rosina Whittle

A new product, an improved maintenance facility, a redesigned IT system, and a different process for orienting new employees: each of these usually comes about as the result of a project. Projects often hold hopes for a better future: a new stream of revenue, more cost-effective operations, employees who have a better grasp of the organization and can contribute more effectively from the start. The project may be large and represent a major expenditure of resources or small where an unsatisfactory outcome is not so visible. A project can mark a step into an unknown, imagined future. Most projects involve an array of stakeholders: people from different departments and disciplines within the project owner's organization and people from consulting firms and other contractors. Stakeholders may include investors or government funders, suppliers, board members, government regulators and permitting agencies, members of the community the project will affect, politicians, people who will use the new facility or product, the sellers and distributors, and many more. The aspirations inherent in projects, the step into the unknown, and the multitude of stakeholders make projects challenging for those who lead them. As aspirations, novelty and complexity rise, so does the challenge. It is easy for project managers to lose their bearings and their competence.

While the felt experience of projects can be marked by disarray, dashed expectations, hurt feelings, and puzzlement, much of the literature on project management focuses on technical aspects of the management of scope, schedule and budget and fairly suppresses the emotional experience. What's lacking is a nuanced discussion of the project environment and an understanding of the complex dynamics of project life. The management theorist Mary Parker Follett defined management practice as 'the art of getting things done by people' (Huff, Tranfield and van Aken 2006: 413). Project managers tend to get things done without much reflection or explicit design, acting directly on the basis of their tacit knowledge, intuition and creativity, honed by experience. They may be exhorted to communicate, communicate, communicate, implying that they can shape projects unilaterally through their experience and common sense. We reject this notion and argue for the valuing of practitioners who bring an understanding of organizational dynamics and design to their practice. Drawing on the idea of management as a design science (Huff, Tranfield and van Aken 2006), we offer some organization design principles to help those managing projects to work more effectively.

We focus on the role of project manager as an insider, charged with managing change from within a temporary organization, a project. We will look at how the organization in the mind (Armstrong 2005) shapes how project managers think about which working practices and relationships are appropriate to the project management task. We describe how the dynamics of task, of time, of turbulence, of tribes and trust, and of transition influence project thinking and practice and offer 15 design principles to help project managers work with these dynamics. We start with our thoughts about projects as organizations.

Projects are organizations, too. This basic idea is easily lost or forgotten. Projects have all the issues and problems of organizations: defining what the task is, how work is controlled and coordinated, who needs what information and when, who talks to whom about what, how performance is judged and by whom, how to change. A project is also temporary; it exists over some pre-specified time. This can exacerbate and compress some of the issues just mentioned or lead to their neglect and avoidance. How necessary is it to deal with these organizational problems if the work is temporary? In contrast to other types of organization, the end is present from the beginning in a project. This can work against fixing organizational problems. We are inclined to put up with otherwise unbearable working relationships and unreasonable task demands if we know they will end in the near future. All too easily, a project can become a small world, in which routines and relationships prevail that would be considered bizarre 'outside'. Changing projects from within this small world is always difficult, sometimes impossible. Common wisdom says it takes a special type of person to be a project manager, perhaps a lion tamer.

We make the case for our thinking by drawing on our different experiences of project work. As a manager, Robin led organizational units that supported a range of major transport and infrastructure projects. Later, she consulted organizations undertaking major capital projects or otherwise seeking to improve supply chain management. Sue has led and been a member of local government and of consulting and university project teams delivering services to internal and external clients. Together with colleagues she has developed and delivered professional development programs to help internal IT, HR, OD and operational project managers lead change in their organizations. We want to raise some issues from our experiences with projects and invite readers to think about their own experiences. We hope our chapter changes the image of a project manager from lion tamer to ring master.

Dynamics that Shape Project Life

Projects generate their own dynamics. We have identified five that are particularly important in shaping project life: the dynamics of task; the dynamics of time; the dynamics of turbulence; the dynamics of tribes and trust; and the dynamics of transition. We discuss these dynamics and offer principles of organization design to help project managers work with them. We think of these principles as heuristics that practitioners can apply to their own situations.

1   THE DYNAMICS OF TASK

Projects can be a response to some organizational imperative, an urgent need to cut costs, address a crisis or failing, or develop a new product or service. Projects can also be a way of life, for IT and other consultants, for those delivering construction and infrastructure developments and to respond to shifting public policy agendas. They can be bigger or more significant than anything an organization or consortium has undertaken before. The tensions and hopes inherent in these sorts of circumstances are felt in the project environment. This is a common scenario in policy implementation when new temporary project organizations are created for a fixed term (one to five years usually) as vehicles to regenerate a locality, to regulate a poorly performing sector, or to renew practices in health, education, welfare, or policing. While the origins of these types of projects can lie in political expediency, we find leaders and managers of project organizations tend to be committed, conscientious and charismatic, the embodiment of hope. All too quickly, this can turn to disappointment and recrimination as the reality of delivering to sky-high expectations kicks in.

The challenge for project managers is to attend to the rational management of a project life cycle while recognizing these tensions and hopes and working with them. The film *The King's Speech* (dir. Tom Hooper, 2010) provides a great example of how a project manager uses a whole range of devices to work with and contain the fear of failure in a high profile project. The film is about Prince Albert, the Duke of York and the second son of King George V. The Prince, who stuttered badly and was painfully shy, lived in his elder brother's shadow. He realized that public address systems and radio were changing how the royal family interacted with the public and that even as a second son, he would have to play an increasingly public role. The later abdication of his brother intensified the pressures on Prince Albert. Speech therapy as we know it today was an unknown discipline. After the failure of several quack therapies, his desperate wife hires Lionel, a failed actor, who helps by using techniques from his theatre training. The speech therapist as project manager deals shrewdly with the daunting nature of the task in several ways. The lessons are in his shabby digs rather than the stiff atmosphere of the palace. He calls the Prince 'Bertie' rather than Your Royal Highness as a way of asserting his authority so the Prince will feel held, and his anxieties contained, by the authority figure. The project manager is allowing his client to lean on him. The Prince has been given the task of speaking to the public as a representative of the royal family, but Lionel sees that the Prince will be overwhelmed and never able to accomplish this normative task if this is how the work is conceptualized. Instead, Lionel, in his role as Project Manager, reframes the task: he tells the Prince to sing what he wants to say or to shout curse words. This reframing helps the Prince gain the self-confidence he needs to deliver a speech by containing the felt anxiety of the normative task, the 'what he should do' (Lawrence 1986). Following his brother's abdication, the Prince ascends to the throne. When the King gives his first wartime speech, the project manager again supports Bertie emotionally by reframing the task. Lionel reconfigures the palace room where the King will make the speech to resemble his shabby digs. He stays in the room in sight of the King, and tells the King to pretend that he's just talking to him. The King delivers the speech in a strong, confident voice – a triumph.

These 'do or die' dynamics of task are felt particularly in complex, 'bet-the-company' projects, which can be gut churning for project managers and participants. They may be at the top of their game professionally and yet can feel at sea in the welter of events. When Christopher O. Ward was named Executive Director of the Port Authority of New York and New Jersey, he found the World Trade Center reconstruction project massively behind schedule and over-budget. He said that the project was sinking under the felt burden of its symbolism and that it had to be turned into an 'ordinary' construction project in order to get done (Dwyer 2011). Those involved in the project (some of whom had lost colleagues in the 9/11 attacks) are likely to have felt a sense of responsibility to reconstruct the Trade Center to honor the dead and also to demonstrate the nation's strength. Feelings like these can be overwhelming and make a task feel impossible (Hirschhorn 1988). Ward recognized this when he decided to use ordinariness as a defense against task anxiety (Trist et al. 1990).

2   THE DYNAMICS OF TIME

Projects are temporary organizations (Graham 1990) brought into existence for an activity that has a defined start and end. The work may require collaboration between people from different organizational units, disciplines and organizations. Some may work on the project full-time, others only part-time. Still others may consult on specific specialist matters at irregular intervals. Some people arrive on day one; others may join and leave at various intervals. Although this can certainly happen in any work situation, its impact is greater in the project environment, where time is constantly in focus. Periodic membership in the project team means working with members who have differentiated knowledge about the project and different levels of commitment. This is a challenge for project managers, who may have lived with a project longer than anyone and forgotten how much they have learned.

They may not recognize the variety of factors that affect the ability of others to join and do effective work. Some participants may be new to the project and just getting their bearings. In a meeting very early on in a project where she was an external subject matter expert working in the project office, Robin felt at a loss when called into a meeting without an announced subject and where she knew only one person of the five or six people scattered around an imposing conference table that could have seated 30 or more. The others weren't introduced and Robin didn't suggest that introductions would be useful. She also felt the pressure of the push for a definitive answer on an issue where it was already apparent there was little agreement. The meeting ended without much accomplished. Robin felt that she lost her competence to a feeling that she *should* know what was happening and was unable to summon skills she had to take up an appropriate role (others may have felt similarly). Without organizational routines as an anchor, people working in projects may struggle to understand who has what role and how to relate to and work with each other. Over time, it can become very difficult for participants to have their voices heard and a challenge for project managers to learn what is known, what is assumed and what is a mystery within their project community. Project managers can find themselves dependent on relatively unknown and perhaps un-trusted others for resources, knowledge, or approvals. Organizational hierarchies, professional politics and work place cultures affect whether, when and how participants are heard.

In the wake of the 1986 Challenger disaster where the shuttle exploded seconds after liftoff, the investigating commission found that six months before the scheduled launch, a Morton Thiokol booster rocket engineer had warned his company of the danger of launching the shuttle in cold weather. The night before the launch date, when it was apparent that the weather would be quite cold, he argued strenuously for a delay in the launch in a conference call with company executives. Morton Thiokol, as the supplier of a critical component, had the authority to postpone the launch. The general manager of Thiokol ultimately told his colleagues 'to take off their engineering hats and put on their management hats'; Thiokol told NASA it was all right to launch. (As reported in *The New York Times* obituary of Roger Boisjoly, the engineer who warned of the shuttle danger; Martin 2012.) Developing the capacity to work with and challenge time as it is perceived by others is a core competence for project managers, as Sue Whittle writes in Chapter 5 of this book. Bringing new project participants 'up to speed' means more than providing them with information about progress against schedule. Managers need to guide people's entry into projects and bring the work on the project into the same time frame for everyone.

3   THE DYNAMICS OF TURBULENCE

Many projects experience difficulties because of turbulence that they are ill equipped to manage (Miller and Lessard 2000). Miller and Floricel (2000) state that turbulence has a quality of surprise and refers to events that are outside the framework that project leaders have envisioned. Accordingly, what constitutes turbulence may differ from project to project. It can arise from events outside of the project, e.g., a new competitor, political factors, a change in technology, or within the project, e.g., bankruptcy of a partner or key supplier, strained relationships among partners, or planning failures. Turbulence can arise when project sponsors are over-optimistic about their capabilities, when firms misjudge the financial risks they are taking on, when new legislation affects the project or regulators make unexpected decisions, or when an owner is unable to close a deal for real estate as planned and cannot give a construction contractor access to the site on the schedule in his contract. In 2008, the World Trade Center redevelopment project was mired in problems: published schedules and budgets were not realistic; 15 major issues critical to the project had not been resolved; there was no effective governance structure; the work was massive, involving multiple buildings and transportation facilities, on a highly constrained site; and the project involved '... 19 public agencies, two private developers, 101 different construction contractors and sub-contractors and 33 different designers, architects and consulting firms ...' (Ward 2008: 5). While the project is perhaps unique in scale, the issues cited will be familiar to those involved in projects of nearly any size and kind: over-optimism regarding schedules and budgets, issues that affect other project phases or participants that don't get decided in a timely way, lack of effective decision-making, and multiple organizations involved not subject to central control, with the possibility that any one of them can act in unexpected ways.

Turbulence can easily cause projects to spiral downward and disintegrate (Miller and Floricel 2000) as parties blame one another and seek to minimize their losses. Panic overtakes thinking. Achieving collective understanding of what is going on is difficult enough in traditional organizations and is all the more difficult in projects where work is not managed tightly from a central control and where multiple organizations are involved (Clegg et al. 2002). Where project managers for owners, contractors, suppliers and other key participants relate to each other principally in a hub-and-spoke, one-on-one basis, they may find the whole hard to see. Group cohesion and appreciation for participants' interdependencies and interests is likely to be lacking. Governance structures provide space for project participants to develop their understanding of the unexpected and create ways to address issues: imagine a giant safety net where the principal players bounce up and down as they try to understand what is happening to the project and them and think about how to address it.

4   THE DYNAMICS OF TRIBES AND TRUST

Project work draws on different groups and organizations and different types of organizations: contractors, suppliers, funders, regulators, investors, clients, consultants and end-users. We become more aware of knowledge and identity boundaries, of differences and disputes, and of self and shared interests as a project unfolds. In project organizations people with a variety of cultures, interests and ways of working are expected to collaborate. Some project staffs may work for firms that usually compete but now are united in a joint venture, as Andrew Day describes in Chapter 1 of this book. Some people may be physically in the same place, while others visit occasionally and at different times, or exist only in virtual space.

The temporary and cross-boundary nature of projects can make it difficult to fully join and connect with one another and with the normative task. This can make for instrumental relations and game-playing, rather than relations of trust, respect and loyalty. Under pressure, it's easy for people to divide the world into us-and-them (Hirschhorn 1998). Saying that a contractor only cares about money is a way of discounting (Mellor and Schiff 1975) the contractor's need for pride in a job well done or the need to be paid in a timely way, and can locate the contractor as a convenient repository of the project's ills.

Some people will feel more a part of the project team than others, perhaps because they have worked together before or they are in the same discipline as the project leader. Others, for example, those whose jobs relate to compliance issues, may find it hard to feel a part of the group because of their work role. The extent to which I feel more 'out' than 'in' can influence how I participate. If my knowledge and experience are valued, I can pitch in and speak with authority. If my contributions are seen as a disruption, or bad news, I might keep my thoughts to myself or perhaps act out the disruptive projections.

Those of us whose work is project-based are used to not having a permanent organization structure to orient ourselves or the luxury of being able to fall into familiar routines when we arrive at our work place each day. People come and go; problems come and go. But we know that we can carry our experiences, our routines and the way we relate to other people with us, from one project to the next. This transference (Hirschhorn 1988) means that it's difficult to step into project work without any history – or baggage. A difficult experience with 'those people' or an unsatisfactory outcome on a past project because of having to compromise might make me defensively alert from the start. On the other hand, I might assume that work will be vetted and approved 'in the usual way' and am puzzled to find different practices in place. Both stereo-typing and dissonance between what I expect or am used to and the surprising situation in a new project can mean that I keep my head down rather than risking criticism or appearing stupid. As each tranche of newcomers shifts loyalties and practices, and each decision point reveals interests and shapes trust, project participants can find that their working relationships change throughout the project's life, at worst ushering in a perpetual Groundhog Day of keeping a low profile. Some may not join the project at all, being there in body but without attachment to the project team. Project participants who stay on the boundary of a project may be choosing to locate their interests and have their identity needs met through an external tribe, such as a professional body, their home organization or department, or client.

One member of a national project team, charged with implementing crime reduction polices across the UK, was very protective of her pre-existing relationships with public housing and police organizations in a particular area. So attached was she that she never fully joined the project team, preferring to relate instrumentally to the work of the project while all the time trying to bend project scheduling and delivery to meet the needs and rhythms of her existing clients. These tribal dynamics, which operate inside, outside and across the project boundary, are often felt as project politics. We may say that someone has 'gone native' or that they 'need to get out more'. They shape the way that project participants and project managers are included and excluded and how they choose to participate or not. Shall I collaborate, comply, speak up, or withdraw (Hirschman 1970)?

Figure 4.1   Dilbert does a project

Source: DILBERT © 2011 Scott Adams. Used by permission of UNIVERSAL UCLICK.

5   THE DYNAMICS OF TRANSITION

The work of a project is to change something from A to B. Understanding the current state, navigating a changing environment, and imagining and planning for a future state are fundamental challenges for project managers. But whose view of the future prevails?

The future can be eagerly anticipated or feared and, as a member of a project team, I may have too much or too little capacity to influence what happens. A production manager was fearful that possible low participation statistics submitted by his factory in the company's current 'improvement through participation' project would threaten his promotion prospects. He decided to massage the figures. He spoke about this with regret and as having to 'defend himself' against 'unrealistic expectations'. His factory was commended.

Imagining a future state is a risky undertaking, inviting and sometimes seducing us to go beyond what we know or what we think is right. When asked to approve the design of a new building, the General Manager (GM) of a new vehicle maintenance facility does not understand what the implications for how work gets done are. The GM is so anxious looking at drawings he doesn't really understand that he approves them, even though he knows that he doesn't understand them. Will the architects assume that the GM has understood the drawings the same way they do and that he is working towards the same future?

The more different and the more numerous are project participants, the more mental models – different images of the way the world works – are in operation and the more possibilities for either misunderstanding or for exciting collaboration (Walsh and Whittle 2009). Different participants may have different definitions for even seemingly standard terms, such as 'estimate at completion'. And for the very reason that 'everyone knows what *that* means', participants may not discover those different meanings for a long time.

In another scenario, a project is charged with replacing stand-alone systems with a new enterprise-wide IT system. Steering committee members decide what functionality is required in the new system. Their departmental affiliations, needs and opinions about what other departments need inevitably influence their images of the future. When the system is ultimately delivered, users may find that features they considered essential in their stand-alone systems don't exist in the new system: their world and that of the designers are not the same. Sue recently had personal experience of this issue when she contracted a firm to refit her shower room, a straightforward time- and cost-bound project. She imagined and specified a pumped shower with enough capacity to give a strong reliable flow. She was aghast and then amused to find the contractor, in his mind fulfilling the brief, had fitted a huge pump more usually found in schools and swimming pools! Project managers need to beware of what seems obvious, both about the future envisaged and how to get there.

As projects progress, the environment changes and projects are all too easily at risk of becoming obsolete before completion. A senior manager in a large London Borough had put her heart and soul into preparing 150 staff to launch a flagship project. This was designed to address significant shortcomings in children's services (for which the Borough had been criticized) and to signal a new start for a service that staff could feel proud of. Two weeks after the launch, national government announced massive funding reductions to these services. The project was left high and dry and the manager was left making decisions about who to make redundant. In turbulent environments (Emery and Trist 1965) the core rationale for a project can suddenly disappear. Project managers can find themselves having to reinvent the future and cope with a transition from hope and commitment to resentment and despair.

Even when a project stays its course, dissenting voices can be heard towards completion, perhaps when it's too late. 'That's not what this project is about' often pops up in projects designed to implement policy where goal posts are changed as emergent (or overlooked) policy agendas are added to project deliverables. A group of 11 city councils was funded by the UK national government to pilot projects to trial new approaches to:

1.   improving the condition of rented housing in their areas; and

2.   reducing unlawful behaviour by landlords through collaboration rather than regulation.

Good working relationships were developing between cities and local landlord organizations in each of the 11 areas. National government clients then announced they wanted each project to supply data on landlords for use in connection with new legislation. This was intended to exclude some landlords from renting out property because they were judged to be 'not a fit person'. This threatened to undermine good relations and trust between landlords and councils and some city councils refused to comply with this late and as they saw it, un-contracted element of the change, even though this meant risking their future funding. A powerful player can try to influence the project so that transition to the future is no longer from A to B but A to C or T.

A tricky scenario for any project manager is when changes go further than people think they have signed on for. Sometimes, the label 'project' disguises the sorts of changes that will be needed for a project to succeed. If people have to change the way they relate to their work and to each other significantly, we think it's better to come clean and talk about organization change, rather than a project. A city transit agency sets up a purchasing project to source new rail cars that are technologically advanced from the current models. The agency project manager knows they cannot maintain the railcars properly unless the agency re-trains its workforce or finds new workers who have the skills to work with the new technology. Calling this 'a railcar purchase' sustains a myth that this is a discrete and simple substitution.

SUMMARY

We have described how the dynamics of task, time, turbulence, tribes and trust, and transition operate in organizations known as projects. We have offered examples of how the dynamics generate problems for those managing project work. Now we suggest 15 design principles to help project managers work with these dynamics and take up roles to contain (Bion 1961) their impact on project success. The relationship of project dynamics to design principles is shown in Figure 4.2.

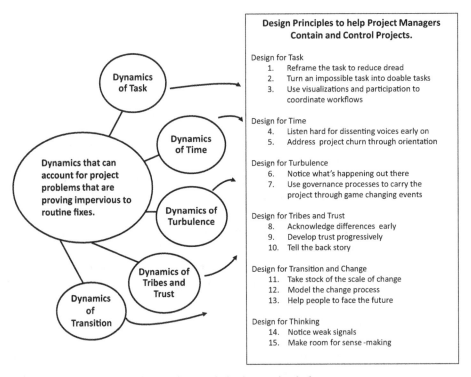

Figure 4.2   **Project dynamics and design principles**

Why Organization Design?

The dynamics of task, time, turbulence, tribes and trust, and transition can be rendered more manageable and their potential impact on project performance reduced if those managing projects:

1.   think of themselves as internal change leaders; and

2.   apply principles of effective organization design to their projects.

Organization design principles inform what is worked on and how. Good design requires artistry and skill in choosing how to adapt principles to fit *this* project for *this* purpose. A design for a cost reduction or a talent retention project in an organization with a highly hierarchical structure will differ from the design of similar projects for a small team of scientists working in virtual space.

Awareness of the design principles can help project managers to anticipate problems before they arise. Emotions associated with belonging and whether I am judged to be an insider or outsider (by myself or others) affect what happens in organizations. Projects, as temporary organizations, can intensify insider/outsider dynamics. These dynamics are rarely addressed in the literature or in project manager development, which stress project cycle issues; the control of scope, schedule and budget; project organization models; teamwork; and communication skills. Project managers on their own are expected to understand project dynamics and develop skills in managing them.

The following principles are intended to help project managers address these dynamics and develop intervention strategies to work with persistent problems that are impervious to technical fixes or extra resources. We hope that collectively they offer a lifeboat to stressed-out project managers as they try to change these temporary organizations from within.

DESIGN FOR TASK

What is the task of the project? Is this a project that *this* team has done before or is this project completely new to everyone involved? Does the project bet the company or threaten some of the stakeholders in some way? A savvy project manager considers this. Where a project means working on a task of huge importance or is overlaid with intense emotion (perhaps because of stirring up the past), the principle is to reframe the task into something doable – the more mundane the better. In *The King's Speech*, the speech therapist reframed the primary task from the terrifying (giving a public address) to helping the Prince gain self-confidence through seemingly silly exercises. He made the task do-able. Using ordinariness as a defense against the anxiety of failure and the dread of not being up to the job is well documented (Trist et al. 1990). *Contain anxieties by reframing the task as one that holds little dread is our first principle.*

When the task of a project is to review a critical incident in a hospital or airport or to work on some other issue with a high emotional charge (such as how to report a failure or how to manage a product contamination), project managers need to make time for project participants to talk openly about their fears and concerns. This reduces the possibility that people will feel overwhelmed and freeze or feel personally responsible for the problem and either take flight or deflect the blame elsewhere (Crombie 1997). (We see extreme examples with the recent suicides associated with the start of the inquiry (another form of project) into the recall of toys from Chinese factories.) In other words, the project manager understands that the normative task (reviewing the incident) must initially give way to the phenomenal task of working through the anxieties (Lawrence 1986). Talking in the open about feelings of anxiety and insecurity does more than help *individuals* regain their sense of competence: it allows group members to relate to each other in different ways as they speak to similar worries and concerns. This may allow the project *group* to work together more freely and to work creatively with ambiguous situations rather than regressing into defensive splitting and projections. *This is our second principle: help people to voice and confront anxieties before asking them to work on a highly charged task.*

How we work to accomplish a project is also an essential element of task. Many projects use diagrams, plans, or mock-ups to show *what* they are creating, but rarely use the same kinds of aids to show *how* they are creating it. When people from different organizational levels worked together to develop project workflows, junior project staff members said it was the only time they had talked with managers about work process. They felt able to ask questions, point out problems, and make suggestions. In essence, the process development sessions were a forum where learning was authorized, and they had a different feel from one-on-one work review sessions with supervisors, where power relationships got in the way of learning. Creating and posting workflows brings work processes into the open. As one manager said when workflows were completed, 'We can see ourselves now'.

One way to start a work process work session is to ask participants to draw the system. We have found that people invariably draw what amounts to a critique of the system. Posting the pictures and doing a gallery walk gives a group a lot of data about disconnects and misunderstandings and the multiple ways that people understand the same processes. *Our third principle: make workflows visible and use participative processes to re-design them.*

DESIGN FOR TIME

Listen hard for dissenting voices on issues related to time is our fourth design principle.
The temporary nature of projects with their continual focus on time can make
it hard for people to speak up when they think the project needs to be slowed
down. The focus on meeting schedules, satisfying political considerations, or
making up for past delays can overwhelm careful consideration of other issues.
Many of us have experience with projects where rushed initial stages resulted
in higher costs later. A corollary of this is *our fifth design principle: think about
the pace of your project, understand where the time should go in your project, and
plan time allocations accordingly.* A large organization conducted an analysis of
major capital project life cycles when it realized that many problems were first
becoming manifest during construction, a phase of the project when addressing
them was costly. Project managers realized that costs often increased where
people whose interests were at stake or with know how were included too
late in the project cycle. They decided to change the pace of the work to make
sure relevant interests are not only represented but also brought in as early as
their interest is at issue. Putting time-in, in the right places, could result in a
reallocation as shown in Table 4.1.

Table 4.1   Reallocation of effort for major capital projects

Effort Then – As % of Project Costs	Activity	Effort Now
2%	Feasibility	5%
8%	Development	20%
90%	Construction	75%

*Acknowledge the passage of time and design some orientation activities to address the
impact of frequently changing project team membership is our sixth design principle.*
A discipline of continuously welcoming people into and orienting them to the
project helps people get up to speed, feel part of the project, and grounded
enough to participate fully. A US-based architect who worked on a project in
the Netherlands noticed that the project manager spent time at each meeting
orienting the architects and engineers who worked on subsystems to the project
as a whole. This included updates on current project status, on decisions made
since the last meeting, on progress on other subsystems, etc. She said that the
design took more time than she was used to for comparable projects in the
US, but the build was smoother and took less time with fewer change orders
than she would have expected on a similar US project. Orientation can take

many forms: distributing meeting agendas, running welcome sessions for newly assigned project staff, convening each meeting by locating the meeting in the project's temporal topography (this is meeting 4 at location L to work on Z); having participants introduce themselves and name their project role if newcomers are present; and inviting clarification about the past if some current project participants were not involved.

DESIGN FOR TURBULENCE

Projects can be swamped by unforeseen events such as supplier problems, funding issues, technology changes that suddenly impact cost parameters or potential market share, or a change in a sponsor's business strategy. Recriminations start and projects spiral downward (Miller and Floricel 2000). Effective project governance structures and techniques help guide actions through stormy environments by supporting communication, cooperation, and decision-making (Miller and Floricel 2000). They should range in complexity and scope according to the size and importance of the project. Governance refers to '… the complex process of steering multiple firms, agencies, and organizations that are both operationally autonomous and structurally coupled in projects through various forms of reciprocal interdependencies (Jessop 1997)[.]' (Miller and Floricel 2000: 135). These processes can be complex for large-scale engineering projects that involve many organizations and stakeholders and smaller-scaled for projects that involve fewer participants. Governance structures and processes slow things down. They give people space to think about 'what' and 'how' without jumping to solutions too fast. They provide a place to develop a collective understanding of issues that arise in the turbulence of the project environment and provide a framework for containing (Bion 1961) and managing polarizing tensions.

Governance defines who has the right and responsibility to make decisions, in consultation with whom and consideration of what. The 2008 assessment of the World Trade Center project's problems recommended the introduction of strong central project governance including '… a Steering authority that can make final decisions about critical path issues, and that will be informed by an organizational structure underneath it that includes all of the stakeholders and allows for meaningful input before decisions are made[.]' (Ward 2008). The aim was to manage the interdependencies of the many construction projects on the tight site. The report also recommended establishment of a more effective structure to manage site logistics as a whole system.

Governance may include practices and processes (Miller and Floricel 2000) that help the parties remember and manage their mutual interests and interdependencies. These might include collaboration between owners and contractors, long-term working relationships, financing arrangements that promote mutuality, and agreements among partners. Owner-contractor collaboration might include regular project meetings of teams of people from both entities where frank discussion is encouraged to establish a norm of joint problem solving. On a project to redesign an employee training process, governance might include regular meetings with project team members and user representatives. A project gateway system, i.e., a planning and review process that includes questions to be answered before a project can enter the next phase, can be a useful project governance mechanism. A first step is a statement of the organizational purpose for the project to help participants keep focused on the overall goal. Well-designed questions then require project managers and organization sponsors to consciously scan the environment at each stage for changes that may influence project outcomes; this may alert them to problems not foreseen at the outset before they become much harder to deal with. A good gateway process is not a paper exercise: an essential component is collective discussion among key participants to determine whether the project should proceed to the next phase: Have all questions been answered satisfactorily? Where answers are problematic, should we proceed anyway with heightened attention to flagged issues? Did something unexpected happen that requires more intensive analysis or management? This process helps participants conceptualize what is happening and better manage project interdependencies. *This is our seventh design principle: design appropriate governance processes to help carry the project through game-changing events.*

DESIGN FOR TRIBES AND TRUST

Tribes push and pull to retain their different interests and ways of doing things. Unmediated, that can make for a cacophony and for difficult relationships. Are the lawyers seen as difficult but useful because they work for the same organization as the owner's engineers whereas the engineers on the contractor's side are seen as stubborn or not bright enough in discussions about construction methods? *Our eighth design principle is: bring tribal affiliations and the interests they represent into the open by acknowledging differences as they affect project work.* Talk about the different points of view, operating procedures and mental models that people bring to the project table as a matter of fact, rather than as a disappointment or failure and talk about them as behaviors and practices rather as personal characteristics. We tend to locate differences in the personal (she's too controlling) or the inter-personal (they just can't get along) rather than in organizational interests (we just can't work how you want us to). Interests are 'predispositions embracing goals, values, desires, expectations that lead a person to act in one way rather than another' (Morgan 1997: 161). Reframing difference as a fact, as ordinary rather than pathological, makes difference more manageable. Rather than being stuck in conflict or avoidance, the recognition of difference opens up the possibility of collaboration and compromise by legitimating a 'third way' (Morgan 1997).

Trust is elusive. It's hard to build and easily dashed. Trust is an element of a group's social capital. It helps 'people to work together for common purposes' (Fukuyama 1995: 1). A project manager needs to build trust between members of a project group or find ways to substitute for it. *Our ninth design principle: create opportunities for project members to work together as much as possible, to develop trust progressively.* It's difficult to develop trust quickly in a room of ten or more people. Early on, trust-building might start with individuals introducing themselves and speaking about their hopes and fears for the project. Speaking is an act of joining. Sharing backgrounds, hopes, and fears builds relationships and trust, as individuals expose their vulnerabilities (Stanford Encyclopedia of Philosophy). The extent to which people reveal themselves is a useful indicator of the 'trust in the room' for any project manager and data about what work needs to be done to build, repair or replace trust.

Putting in place transparent controls, being clear about priorities and practice protocols, and having access to well understood and good enough dispute procedures are mechanisms for addressing an absence or lack of trust, particularly at the start of projects.

Over the project life cycle, the status of trust will change, as relationships are formed, undermined and broken. Trust means I think you will not take advantage of me for your own ends, even if you have the opportunity to do so (Yuki et al. 2005). But sometimes history can get in the way. Project managers need to be alert to both transferences from the past and shifts in trust in the present in order to intervene appropriately, as projects develop.

On an IT development project, the newly hired project manager felt that he couldn't do anything without his boss breathing down his neck. It was only much later that he found out that the last major IT project his boss was involved with had been a disaster. If his boss had mentioned that before and they had been able to talk about it, they may have been able to develop a more productive way of working. *Our tenth principle is make it a practice to disclose the back-story.* The story that explains my puzzling behavior, or the way 'that person' always reacts, may have fallen out of awareness, forgotten as a conscious influence shaping attitudes to work, people and problems. If a project manager can find a way to ask the question 'What's going on around here? This is the second (third, fourth) time this has happened', it signals that a pattern has been noticed and that I need to account for my recurring behaviour. The risk is that what's seen as a problematic pattern may say more about me than about those exhibiting the behaviour! As Freud said, sometimes a cigar is just a cigar.

DESIGN FOR TRANSITION AND CHANGE

Our eleventh principle: take stock of what your project really is – an incremental transition or fundamental organizational change? If the latter, come to grips with that, call it that and undertake all that is necessary to bring about organizational change. Over-simplification causes people to miss what is really going on (Weick and Sutcliffe 2007).

How can project managers lead the change that unfolds in any transition? The first challenge is to understand how broad, how deep and how radical the changes are. Next, appreciate that even when change is desired, it involves a loss of the familiar. People find themselves losing their sense of mastery, which can be unsettling for professionals who pride themselves on their competence (Marris 1986). Change can be bewildering and resistance is an understandable reaction. Help project participants recognize the changes they are going through and understand the nature of those changes by providing some educational input about change processes. *Offer some way of modeling and thinking about the process of change to help people through it, is our twelfth design principle.*

Project managers need to help people see the future and make what they see visible to each other is our thirteenth design principle. Understanding the implications of the future requires a good understanding of the present state: what it is, who will give up something in the future state and what that will mean to them. Seeing the future is easier in projects producing artifacts such as a building or infrastructure or a report. For projects with less tangible outputs, such as a change in staffs' behaviour or improved relations with suppliers, visualizing what that looks like, feels like and sounds like is more difficult. Using the five senses to grab hold of a fuzzy future can be fun and done quickly and double as an orientation activity.

DESIGN FOR THINKING

Information doesn't come to a project from someone running into a meeting saying, 'Listen everyone. Something has been brewing that is of critical importance to us. The four stakeholders involved have different views of the situation. This is what it all means to the project'. Instead, information is often ambiguous. A statement may have several meanings or have ambiguous implications. The budget officer may report that project contingency is at 4 per cent. To some that means that the project is in critical shape; others may almost not hear the report. Projects run into trouble when work is so routinized that changes are not noticed, when we mindlessly go with the flow. *Notice weak signals is our fourteenth design principle.* Weick and Sutcliffe (2007) write about the importance of paying attention to weak signals: to notice that something, like an incremental slowdown in deliveries or invoice reviews, is a little different and to wonder what it means. They caution to wear one's expectations lightly, noting the paradox that while our expectations help us make sense of events, they can also choke off recognition of what is actually happening.

OD consultants had designed and run a new development program for a client for three years. The client wanted to run the program as an in-house offer and a transitional project group was tasked with bringing in-house people up to speed on their competencies on program design and management. Work began on program 4 as a project, with consultants making their thinking and practices available to Jane and Tom who would be directing the program in-house in program 5. Gradually, consultants' 'reasonable requests' for information about intended program aims and selling points were met with disinterest, delays and avoidance. Attributing this behaviour to over work and the novelty of the situation, consultants continued to mentor Jane and Tom and hand over roles and responsibilities. It came as a shock when Tom acted unilaterally, refusing to deliver the program to the existing design and took it in a different direction. Consultants had blotted out how authority relations between themselves and Tom and Jane needed to change in order for the project to be a success and did not pick up on the weak signals that these changes were happening.

Our fifteenth design principle: make room for sense-making. Sense-making happens when people make time for understandings and views to emerge. Sense-making helps uncover assumptions and meanings and misunderstandings. It can occur in informal conversation or in orientation meetings such as the ones the project manager in the Netherlands held. It happens when someone sends an email noting what they understood from a meeting and the implications for follow-on work. It happens best when project participants feel able to participate fully, when people are able to air doubts and differences, when trust has been developed. This is probably not a familiar scenario. So look to people with diverse backgrounds and varied relationships to the project (a new person, someone who is matrixed, a stakeholder, a sceptic). They can be very helpful to puzzled project apparatchiks as they may be tuned into different interpretations and ways of making sense of what's happening not available to project stalwarts.

Conclusion

In writing this chapter we have experienced the budget overruns and rework characteristic of project life. We have worked together previously in different relationships but we have never written together. With a clear and useful chapter specification, we have still found our past has shaped how we have worked on our tasks and how we have worked with each other. Our cultural differences and identities have informed debates on the use of language, style and substance, and our differences have sometimes been played out by one or the other keeping a low profile. We have known from the beginning that we just need to accommodate each other long enough and well enough to see the project through so we haven't bottomed some of our disputes. Maybe neither of us has admitted that each of us has had to do more than we signed on for? The dynamics of projects cannot be eradicated, only worked with.

Traditionally, support for managers has offered ways to clarify and control tasks and provided advice about how to lead and motivate project teams to generate commitment (Cobb 2012). We have offered an organization design approach to help project managers tune into and appreciate some of the more pervasive project dynamics. These relate to task uncertainty, time and temporariness, turbulence, tribes and trust, and transition. We think of project managers as charged with leading change from within to secure successful project outcomes and subject to the sorts of pressures and dilemmas our co-authors have written about. The temporary nature of project organizations intensifies these pressures and dilemmas such that those responsible for steering the work of project teams can easily become overwhelmed. By helping project managers and their communities of practice (Lave and Wenger 1998) better understand what's happening here and now, a design approach enables insiders to recover their competence and collaborate as professionals during the project's life. Why wait for the project post mortem? We hope that this chapter offers you some ideas to make sense of your own projects.

References

Armstrong, D. 2005. *Organization in the Mind: Psychoanalysis, Group Relations, and Organizational Consultancy*, edited by R. French. London: Karnac (Books) Ltd.

Clegg, S.R. et al. 2002. Governmentality matters: Designing an alliance culture of inter-organizational collaboration for managing projects. *Organization Studies*, 23(3), 317–37.

Cobb, A. 2012. *Leading Project Teams: The Basics of Project Management and Team Leadership*. Second Edition. London: Sage.

Crombie, A. 1997. Active maladaptive strategies, in *The Social Engagement of Social Science: A Tavistock Anthology. Volume 3: The Socio-Ecological Perspective*, edited by E. Trist, F. Emery and H. Murray. Philadelphia, PA: University of Pennsylvania Press, 115–35.

Dwyer, J. 2011. Returning Ground Zero to New Yorkers. *The New York Times* [Online, 9 August]. Available at: http://www.nytimes.com/2011/08/10/ny region/returning-ground-zero-to-new-yorkers.html [accessed: 24 April 2012].

Emery, F.E. and Trist, E.L. 1965. The causal texture of organizational Environments. *Human Relations*, 18(Feb), 21–32.

Fukuyama, F. 1995. *Trust: The Social Virtues and the Creation of Prosperity*. New York: The Free Press.

Graham, R.J. 1989. *Project Management as if People Mattered*. Bala Cynwyd, PA: Primavera Press.

Hirschhorn, L. 1988. *The Workplace Within: Psychodynamics of Organizational Life*. Cambridge, MA, and London: The MIT Press.

Hirschman, A.O. 1970. *Exit, Voice, and Loyalty: Responses to Decline in Firms, Organizations, and States*. Cambridge, MA: Harvard University Press.

Huff, A., Tranfield, D. and van Aken, J.E. 2006. Management as a design science mindful of art and surprise: A conversation between Anne Huff, David Tranfield and Joan Ernst van Aken. *Journal of Management Inquiry*, 15(4), 413–24.

Lave, J. and Wenger, E. 1998. *Communities of Practice: Learning, Meaning, and Identity*. Cambridge: Cambridge University Press.

Lawrence, W.G. 1986. A psychoanalytic perspective for understanding organizational life, in *When the Twain Meet: Western Theory and Eastern Insight in Exploring Indian Organizations*, Chattopadhyay, G., Gangee, Z., Hunt, L. and Lawrence, W.G. Allahabad: Wheeler & Co.

Marris, P. 1986. *Loss and Change*. Revised Edition, reprinted in 1993 and 1996. London and New York: Routledge.

Martin, D. 2012. Roger Boisjoly, 73, Dies; Warned of Shuttle Danger. *The New York Times* [Online, 3 February]. Available at: http://www.nytimes.

com/2012/02/04/us/roger-boisjoly-73-dies-warned-of-shuttle-danger.html [accessed: 24 April 2012].

Mellor, K. and Schiff, E. 1975. Discounting. *Transactional Analysis Journal*, 5(3), 295–302.

Miller, R. and Lessard, D. 2000. Public goods and private strategies: Making sense of project performance, in *The Strategic Management of Large Engineering Projects: Shaping Institutions, Risks, and Governance*, edited by R. Miller and D.R. Lessard. Cambridge, MA: MIT Press, 19–49.

Miller, R. and Floricel, S. 2000. Building governability into project structures, in *The Strategic Management of Large Engineering Projects: Shaping Institutions, Risks, and Governance*, edited by R. Miller and D.R. Lessard. Cambridge, MA: MIT Press, 131–50.

Morgan, G. 1997. *Images of Organization*. Thousand Oaks, CA: Sage.

Stanford Encyclopedia of Philosophy available on line at: http://plato.stanford. edu/entries/trust/ [accessed: 3 June 2012].

The King's Speech (dir. Tom Hooper, 2010).

Trist, E., Higgin, G., Murray, H. and Pollock, A. 1990. The assumption of ordinariness as a denial mechanism: Innovation and conflict in a coal mine, in *The Social Engagement of Social Science: A Tavistock Anthology, Volume I: The Socio-Psychological Perspective*, edited by E. Trist and H. Murray. Philadelphia, PA: The University of Pennsylvania Press, 476–93.

Walsh, M. and Whittle, S.R. 2009. When consultants collaborate and when they do not: Some reflections on experience and practice, in *Mind-ful Consulting*, edited by S. Whittle and K. Izod. London: Karnac.

Ward, C. 2008. World Trade Center Assessment. New York: Port Authority of New York and New Jersey. Available at: http://graphics8.nytimes.com/ packages/pdf/nyregion/city_room/20080630_WTCAssessmentBookFF.pdf [accessed: 15 July 2012].

Weick, K.E. and Sutcliffe, K.M. 2007. *Managing the Unexpected: Resilient Performance in an Age of Uncertainty*. 2nd Edition. San Francisco, CA: John Wiley & Sons, Inc.

Yuki, M., Maddux, W., Brewer, M. and Takemura, K. 2005. Cross-cultural differences in relationship- and group-based trust. *Personality and Social Psychology Bulletin*, 31(1), 48–62.

Quick, Quick, Slow: Time and Timing in Organizational Change

Susan Rosina Whittle

Introduction

It's all too easy to think of time as a constant, flowing past endlessly at the same rate. Billions of years ago, the earth had a five hour day but the impact of an asteroid, that created the moon and its gravitational field, has been slowing down our planet ever since. The 24-hour day is only relevant to our time, the present. Now days are getting shorter again, as the moon moves away from the earth. In the future, a 24-hour day will seem bizarre. There is no absolute measure of time (Vimal and Davia 2010). When people in organizations think and behave as if time is a given, they share assumptions about what happens when and at what pace. These time logics (Reay and Hinings 2009) indicate that time is an aspect of the culture of that organization that people are attached to. Time logics can preclude thinking and behaving in different and more effective ways (Schein 1985).

An experienced and well respected doctor of public health had led a strategic restructuring of community health services across a city. This relocated nursery nurses, health visitors, and others away from surgeries provided by local family doctors into locality-based groups, resourced according to levels of deprivation and indicators of community (ill) health. The changes ran into difficulty when the local doctors realized they would lose some of their staff and might have to take on more service provision themselves. They did not feel fully consulted on the restructuring, which they accused of being policy-driven rather than evidence-based. They felt things had not been handled in the right order or at the right pace. They were hurried. Inter-professional relations nosedived and a sensible strategy became a political battlefield. If only the implementation rewind button could be pressed back a couple of months, when some concerns were expressed but side-lined by prioritizing the need to meet end of year reporting cycles. The doctor didn't want to spend any more time on this and brought in an external consultant.

When we talk about the work of crafting organizational change, time is often an issue. There is never enough time. Decisions are taken too slowly or too quickly. The planning workshop was hurried to meet the contract deadline. A feedback presentation is brought forward, because the CEO won't be around next week. Things don't happen when agreed or there is obsessive clinging to the timing of events and actions as if to a life boat in a stormy sea. Blame can be directed at the client, who is accused of naive haste, or the consultant, willfully delaying the next phase of a change project. So why do time and pace rarely feature as significant factors in the literature on organizational change (Huy 2001)?

Orchestrating the sequencing, pace and tempo of interventions is a core competence for practitioners of organizational change. Whilst external consultants can develop this competence on the job, it is perhaps more difficult for internal consultants and change agents to learn by doing, because they are artifacts of their own organizations. I will refer to internal consultants and change agents (those who act to change organizations of which they are members) as 'insiders'. Finding ways to be more mind-ful (Whittle 2009) of the use and abuse of time in their client organizations and in their own working practices can help insiders to work in ways that are more 'timely'. In this chapter, I describe what to look for to diagnose problems related to time and offer some thoughts and lessons from experience to inform practice. I cannot claim to offer a theory but hope that these thought experiments (Weick 1995) will contribute to the development of a theory of time in organization change. But first, a few words about how organizational time is experienced.

Experiencing Organizational Time

Changing relationships to time frequently involves changing culture, those well-established routines and practices that structure organization life. For example, changing from an experienced-based to an evidence-based approach to decision-making can slow down planning and action cycles, often in ways that some find unbearable. Introducing on-line booking for health appointments or hotel rooms requires access to real time data and the development of operational and management routines that can supply that data. Current time logics can be difficult to challenge and may be contested. 'The quicker the better' may be a useful mantra and held by both company and customers in a fast food or travel business, but anyone visiting a doctor or hairdresser will know that challenging time logics to get the timing right is a tricky business.

Whilst customers have some choice about patronizing organizations that consume too much of their time or give too little consideration to their time, many working in organizations feel that they have no choice. Compliance with the prevailing logic seems like the only option. So, we resent feeling at the beck and call of a boss who thinks that her time is the only time that matters or being time-jacked by a corporate change agenda that offers us few if any real benefits. Noticing whose time is valued and whose is not is a good first indicator of an organization's temporal culture.

Our sense of organizational time and of appropriateness of pace is also produced in day-to-day experiences. We speak of time flying by or dragging depending on what we are doing. A journey on a new road will always seem longer. As I look for signposts and follow the twists and turns, I am unsure whether I am travelling in the right direction. With familiarity, time is shortened. James, a process improvement specialist in a manufacturing plant, spoke to me about how a production worker can find spending a whole day at a meeting very tiring and can struggle to maintain engagement. James describes his role as a change agent whose task 'is surely to make the unfamiliar familiar so the change journey is shortened'. Careful attention to the design of events, for example by employing a range of learning styles, task structures and group formations, can help to speed up familiarization.

We think of time as perishable: it is lost if not used now and wasted if not used well. These anxieties about the use of time may be distributed randomly but it is more likely that they occur in patterns, being concentrated in different departments, in different jobs, locations, tasks, ages, genders and other organizational categories. Experiential mapping of time can offer intriguing insights into an organization's temporal cultures. But, be cautious. Time is relative. It can pass quickly (or very slowly) depending 'which side of the bathroom door you're on' (Zall's Second Law, quoted in Wittman 2009). Also, we are very good at locating a time problem in someone else: they are taking too long to agree a plan; it would help if you slowed down a bit; you might have all the time in the world but I have to meet a deadline; I can't believe they haven't done that yet. Realizing that different people inhabit different time worlds, at different times and in different contexts, and that these are as legitimate as my time worlds can be a revelation when working to change organizations.

Time is money and many devices are designed to control what happens when. Project aims and specifications, Gantt charts, meeting schedules and the rhythms of resource planning (who does what) attempt the 'material anchoring of quantified time intervals in cognitive artifacts' (Hutchins 2005; Fauconnier and Turner 2008). Even so, organizational change can often overrun its schedule or stall altogether, as intentions become caught up in the internal tempos of client organizations. All too easily, waiting (for meetings to be rescheduled, contracts negotiated, information to be available, and events to be organized) can become the norm. Who controls time is therefore a critical influence on organizational change. Metaphorically, this is likely to be the person on the inside of the bathroom door with power given away by anyone desperate to make use of the facilities. Signaling that you are needy is likely to be interpreted as powerlessness and you and your change initiative will spend a lengthy and frustrating time outside the bathroom door. 'In essence the trick is always to introduce change with the air of someone sitting on the proverbial throne' (Billy O'Shea personal communication).

SEQUENCING, TEMPO AND IMPROVISATION

How different groups and individuals experience time in *their* organizational lives shapes interest in change and resistance to change. If there aren't enough hours in a day, then joining a transformation team is unlikely to appeal. Likewise, if you have worked at your own steady pace for years, why should you suddenly march along to a tune played by someone else? To address these dynamics, it is essential to understand current relationships to time in your client organization and to work to change these relationships. Three helpful ideas are sequencing, tempo and improvisation.

Planned change often requires insiders to work on shifting an organization's macro relationship with time, say from being stuck in the past to a concern for the future (Sama 2009). Following the financial crisis, CEO's, Organization Development (OD) and Human Resource (HR) specialists in banks are engaged in this type of work, which means reducing head count and redesigning reward practices. But the pace of change is not quick enough for taxpayers and those hit by spending cuts. Why does change take so long? Banks and governments respond by saying now is not 'the right time' to reduce salaries and bonuses as this might jeopardize banks' abilities to retain the best people and the banks' abilities to pay back their huge public loans.

The idea of 'a right time' employs an implicit sequencing of events and actions that are judged to be appropriate for the agenda for change. Sequencing refers to how the different steps, stages and interventions that are part and parcel of organizational change relate to one another, along with rationales about why they are sequenced in this or that way. The 'why' is crucial. Rationales offered by your client provide insights into their model of time. Aspects of sequencing that you find obvious, surprising, uncomfortable or just plain wrong, offer insights into your own model of time.

Sequencing can be by resource time (three months for step 1, nine months for step 2, six weeks for step 3), calendar time (in May, in June, in September) or progressive time (first we need to do X and then we can move on to Y).

External consultants, who come with tried and tested proprietary models of organizational change, are used to defending why stage 1 is followed by stages 2 and 3, just as night follows day. They carry their time frames and their sequencing logic with them, frequently unchallenged. As a result, change can feel like the pearl in an oyster, beautifully crafted but still a foreign body. I believe that failure to work with organizational time is one reason for the limited success of much outsider-led planned change. Often, momentum is difficult to build and is 'lost' when outsider consultants exit, as the intensity of change reverts to its usual pace. Insiders can design much more time-resonant and impactful intervention strategies. By making opportunities to explore their own and their clients' assumptions about sequencing and intervening to change those assumptions, insiders can be much more effective in mobilizing and sustaining change.

In his chapter in this book, Andrew Day describes his work as an internal, consulting to an alliance between two global organizations to design and produce engines. He recounts how he intervened to temporarily suspend unhelpful rules-of-the-game which dictated the ineffective approach to decision making employed by his client organization. The sequence of activities used in the intervention is shown clearly in his Figure 1.2 (see page 38). Here is his rationale:

> We felt it was too risky and pragmatically difficult to get [different business units] together as a group. We hypothesised that this would stir up too much anxiety which would heighten the competitive power dynamics between the different business units. We therefore chose to meet separately with each of them to contain their level of anxiety (Winnicott 1971) and that of the alliance managers. (Day: 37, Chapter 1, this book)

This progressive sequencing took six months, much slower than the client's usual pace.

In addition to sequencing, two more dimensions of time to keep in mind when working as an insider are tempo and improvisation.

Tempo refers to choices about whether organizational change is relaxed or driven, with a constant or varied pace and single or multiple rhythms. Is the tempo designed in waltz time, constant and not too demanding, or more akin to a boot-camp march or rave? Speeding up and slowing down the pace of a restructure or introduction of new technology can happen without changing the underlying tempo. A waltz can be faster or slower. A change of tempo means altering the basic rhythm of change (dancing to a different beat) and this can be useful to signal different stages in a planned sequence (a large group event or launch, for example) and the entry of a new group of change agents, say frontline supervisors, IT or corporate communications specialists. Frequently, the pace of organizational change is expected to speed up as implementation descends through the hierarchy, with Directors having months of preparation and front line service staff and operators receiving a one or two day training session, if that. Having waited outside the corporate change bathroom door, this can be experienced as an inappropriately short time to do what needs to be done.

Time is one of the design principles in Stevens' and Whittle's chapter on managing projects (Chapter 4). The tempo and pace of work varies across the different streams of project work, across professional specialisms and over the project life cycle. All too easily, too slow or too fast a pace can become the norm, such that project managers are faced with intervening to catch up or scrambling to bring new people on board. Contractors join a project at different times and are expected to hit the ground running. Finding ways to relax the tempo temporarily, to help people come up to speed through induction and orientation sessions, can support a faster working pace later.

The third dimension is improvisation and refers to opportunities for expressive timing, when individuals and groups in your client system can choose to come in earlier or later than planned or play a little longer than scripted. Insiders may choose to repeat some steps in the sequence of change activities because of unintended benefits or because later work has challenged their validity. A stage may have to be jettisoned when a pilot program proves it to be superfluous or a chance conversation reveals the need to rewrite the closing score or the opening solo. The more organizational change depends on the participation of organization members, the greater the need for improvisation.

An internal OD consultant had been working for a day and a half with a group of departmental managers charged with analyzing what went wrong and what to do about a recent product problem. Discussion flipped between polite agreement about causes and actions to lightly veiled accusations of incompetence, 'not-me' behaviour, and withdrawal. In two hours, everyone would be leaving. The members of this group had learned well how to talk themselves out of time for completing a task. The consultant could join in this defensive routine (Argyris 1986) which uses limited time resources as a device for maintaining the status quo. Choosing to improvise, the OD consultant decided to tear up the usual closing script, where she would step into an expert role and 'solve' the problem at hand, and spoke instead to the pattern of behaviour that usually occurred round about this time. She suggested that, as useful work seemed to have come to a halt, the group should disband now and reconvene tomorrow, as things might look different in the morning light. The sense of shock was palpable and the group completed their task in the two hours remaining. But even so, was the consultant nevertheless trapped in her client system's time logic? Who decides, and on what basis, that almost two days gives the right time and tempo to do this work? Could the work have been done in one day, or half a day?

Such questions require a way to mindfully interrogate how organizational practices not only take time for granted but rely on time to defend against change. Constructing a model of 'time in the mind', comprising sequencing, tempo and improvisation, can help insiders get in touch with their own model(s) of time as well as those in their organization (Sandelands and Stablein 1987). These are shown in Figure 5.1 on the following page (adapted from Honing 2001).

Problems with Time and Timing and How to Work with Them

Problems with time and timing can be about the sequencing and tempo of planned change and opportunities, or the lack of opportunities for improvisation. In my experience, many of these issues are about intervention design. The extent to which an insider does or does not draw on local and timely knowledge and their (perhaps implicit) understanding of their client system to craft a design fit for purpose can be a critical factor in an intervention.

Figure 5.1   Time-in-the-mind

Bearing in mind local time zones can help to ensure an intervention design is fit for purpose. Try to identify the time zones in your organization and ensure that the design does not disenfranchise whole groups of people from participation because of when they work (the night shift or weekends), when they go on holiday (avoid significant change over the summer or Christmas vacation periods), or because their working time is away from base (drivers, sales staff). Be aware of those people who will need to make a difficult choice between time spent participating in change and time working (on the hospital ward, in the classroom, on the reception desk) to explore whether rethinking sequencing, tempo or improvisation can address their dilemma. Time boundaries can be physical (night and day, Greenwich Mean Time), contractual (hours worked) and psychological ('working time is for my patients'). These boundaries can signal different time worlds. A friend who works the night shift in airport operations describes how organizational groups that are in conflict on the day shift are not at night because the full panoply of management is not there at night and people work things out. So time can influence what the problem is and how it is felt. Insiders need to use their intimate 'here and now' knowledge of their client systems to avoid these kinds of issues.

A common sequencing problem is not working on the right thing at the right time. In the current economic climate, a local government HR consultant had to work with his client system's sense that changes to improve productivity were 'a waste of time' as many managers felt they were on the hit list for closure. Those managers already inhabited a future that rendered the here and now task of productivity improvement irrelevant. Being aware of the client's time frame (the present, the past or the future) helps to avoid a time misfit. This can happen when an insider is trying to work on a presenting task (whether planning for a technology change, improving quality, or restructuring teams) when those involved have regressed to the past or taken flight to the future. Many triggers can evoke these dynamics, including the client's previous experiences with the insider, whether that's a CEO or a change specialist. A timely intervention will be designed to contain the client (Grueneisen and Izod 2009) and internal consultant and bring both into the present before working on the presenting task. In more challenging environments and with shorter business cycles, I have found this increasingly relevant when supporting insider led change. As insiders have to live with their past efforts, because they cannot exit their client systems, unfinished business or unresolved difficulties from previous interventions can easily derail current work.

Two other well-known scenarios that get the timing wrong are diagnosing before contracting and intervention before diagnosis. As organization members, insiders can be seduced into working collusively, diagnosing prematurely and intervening impulsively, rather than working developmentally with their client organization. Andrew Day's chapter in this book describes how these dynamics shaped his experiences as an OD consultant working inside a manufacturing company. The consulting cycle (Kolb and Frohman 1970) offers a road map of the sequencing of planned change and is invaluable in helping insiders to stay on course and avoid working on the right thing at the wrong time.

Even the most competent insiders sometimes find that organizational changes generate significant anxieties in themselves. This can happen when the changes are very political, when they require the use of skills and approaches in which insiders are less experienced, or when success is difficult to measure. In these situations, the appeal of using 'on-time' and perhaps 'on-budget', as a security blanket for good work and as indicators of success, can be very strong. Is it better to be later and effective or on time and have little impact? Testing whether I can ask this question of myself and then whether I dare risk asking the same question to my client are good indicators of whether I am a time lord or time victim.

Not all apparently time-related problems need time-based interventions. Insiders will be more than familiar with working with groups (of managers, trainees, boards, project teams, crisis teams, department heads, professionals, etc.) that seem to become stuck (Critchley and Casey 1989) and struggle to work on the task for which they are convened. Inexplicably large amounts of time are spent unproductively as members argue, withdraw, lead, undermine and collude with each other. Bion describes such groups as operating in basic assumption mode where 'references to time have no meaning' (Bion 1961: 172). They have 'a disturbed relationship to time' in which all 'activities that require an awareness of time are imperfectly comprehended and tend to arouse feelings of persecution' (Bion 1961: 158–9). Frustration and anxiety rise as task work seems impossible to complete. It is unlikely that changes to sequencing and tempo will have much impact here. As in the scenario described at the start of this chapter, an insider improvisation that goes 'off-script' is required to reconnect members of the group with reality, including time. Taking up a temporary role of process consultant (Schein 1998) can help authorize insiders to intervene effectively in these kinds of situations.

Basic assumption behaviour arises from unconscious anxiety about organizational change. Explicit delays to scheduled meetings, information releases, or authorizations to spend; direct challenges to your methods or knowledge that demand 'we go back to the beginning'; or compliant silence might be better thought of as resistance (Block 1981). Block describes 'a sure clue for resistance is when you hear the same idea explained to you for the third time. Or when you hear yourself answering the same question for the third time' (Block 1981: 164). Having a good sense of timing is essential to working with resistance. You can't work with yesterday's resistance today. It needs to be worked with in the moment. Block advises naming the resistance when it occurs, by saying 'You don't seem to think the methods I am using are appropriate' for example. This should be followed by silence, to enable your client (or sometimes your colleague) to take responsibility for their resistant behaviour. This can be more risky for an insider who might not have the authority to choose the methods or techniques employed in a corporate change. If that's the case, maybe it's time to move on.

Working with Time and Timing are Core Competences

Knowing how to orchestrate the tempo and sequencing of organizational change and being able to improvise appropriately and in a timely manner are core competences for insider consultants and change leaders. I believe that this applies more to insiders than outsiders for a number of reasons.

Insiders rarely scout or contract explicitly for organizational change work. At best, entry and exit boundaries are unclear. If you are a senior manager or CEO leading change, they may not exist at all. As one insider said 'you are just there'. Insiders cannot rely on beginnings and endings for boundary containment. They have to make their own time boundaries by devising routines and rituals that remind them and signal to their clients that a boundary is being crossed. Insiders who fail to mark entry and exit boundaries risk getting lost.

Insider change is often imposed from the top down and the need for difficult work can remain unacknowledged or addressed only tangentially while working on something else more palatable or less confrontational. Opportunities for and expectations about any diagnostic work tend to be influenced by who you are and where you are in the hierarchy, rather than your authority in role. Without tempo, sequencing and improvisation skills, insiders can spend their organizational lives playing other people's tunes.

This is because, as a member of the same organization, insiders are inextricably linked with their client systems in ways that outsiders are not. For example, an insider is likely to share a sense of shame about poor performance or dangerous practices where an outside consultant is more able to maintain distance and thus be more helpful to her client (Schein 1998). In 2009, this happened following events in a UK hospital where many patients died of neglect. The independent Healthcare Commission described management as 'being obsessed' with hitting targets and cutting costs while patients went unattended over a three-year period. The question asked was 'How could this go on for so long?' Internal consultants were no longer seen as trustworthy, and indeed doubted their own professional judgment. External expertise was brought in.

Being inside, insiders need to work at distinguishing their responsibilities for success and failure from their clients' responsibilities. By thinking about organizational change as comprising time-bounded projects, insiders can avoid becoming lost in their own organizations and complicit in timeless obsessions and delusions. Mind-ful awareness of one's own preferred sequences and tempos for change helps to defend against collusion with your client's time-in-the-mind and offers the prospect of better thought-through and more impactful change from the inside.

Conclusion

'When' tends to come somewhere behind the 'what, how and who' questions that are usually brought to mind when designing organizational changes. Insiders can find it difficult to challenge the pace and rhythms of their own organizations. Whilst explicit contracting and the fee payment schedule help external consultants to retain their own sense of timing, the potential for program slippage and drift is greater with insider-led change. Some insiders struggle to complete planned change programs at all. Even if the program is sustained, the possibility of being swept along or becalmed by your own organization is ever present, as insiders feel unable to name the problematic pace or sequence and do not have the external's advantage of being able to exit.

I have argued that an understanding of time, as an aspect of client culture and as a model in my own head, can help internal consultants and change agents understand some of the problems they encounter. These include a sense of being out of step of; of marching to a different rhythm; and of being in the chorus line rather than orchestrating interventions (Kenton et al. 2003). These can be mitigated by working in a more timely way if I am aware of my own models of time. This is in keeping with Huy who proposes that large scale organizational change requires 'temporally capable change agents to mindfully juxtapose multiple intervention types while attending to multiple conceptions of time' (Huy 2001: 610). Because insiders inhabit (Bourdieu 1984) their organizations, they have more opportunities to calibrate their organization's relationship to time and work iteratively with issues of sequencing, pace and improvisation.

Modeling time-in-the-mind, of both the insider and client organization, offers cognitive artifacts (Hutchins 2005) to anchor perceptions and experiences of time within plans for change. The process of looking inside oneself to access one's own constructions of 'the right time' and to work with feelings of lateness, haste and a waste of time, are integral to understanding time in clients' systems. Unlike sight and sound, we have no sensory organ to detect time (Bluedorn 2002). There are quantum differences between clock time and time as experienced by you or me. Understanding that 'Perceived time … represents the mental status of the beholder' (Wittman 2009) is crucial when changing organizations from within.

Acknowledgements

My thanks to Mary Rafferty (Organization Development Consultant), Bill O'Shea (Operational Excellence & Operations Support Director) and Lisa Gardiner (Senior Consultant, Organization Development) for their observations and comments on an early draft of this chapter.

References

Argyris, C. 1986. Reinforcing organizational defensive routines: An unintended human resources activity. *Human Resource Management*, 25(4), Winter, 541–55.

Bion, W. 1961. *Experiences in Groups and Other Papers*. London: Tavistock Publications.

Block, P. 1981. *Flawless Consulting: A Guide to Getting Your Expertise Used*. San Francisco, CA: Jossey-Bass.

Bluedorn, A.C. 2002. *The Human Organization of Time: Temporal Realities and Experience*. Stanford, CA: Stanford University Press.

Bourdieu, P. 1984. *Distinction: A Social Critique of the Judgement of Taste*. Cambridge, MA: Harvard University Press.

Critchley, B. and Casey, D. 1989. Organizations get stuck too. *Leadership and Organization Development Journal*, 10(4), 3–12.

Grueneisen, V. and Izod, K. 2009. Power dynamics of expertise and containment in the process of hiring and being hired, in *Mind-ful Consulting*, edited by S. Whittle and K. Izod. London: Karnac Books, 57–74.

Fauconnier, G. and Turner, M. 2008. Rethinking metaphor, in *The Cambridge Handbook of Metaphor and Thought*, edited by Ray Gibbs. Cambridge: Cambridge University Press, 53–66.

Hutchins, E. 2005. Material anchors for conceptual blend. *Journal of Pragmatics*, 37, 1555–77.

Huy, Q.N. 2001. Time, temporal capability, and planned change. *The Academy of Management Review*, 26(4), 601–23.

Kenton, D.M. and Taylor, B. 2003. *The Role of the Internal Consultant*. Roffey Park Institute, UK.

Kolb, D.A. and Frohman, A.L. 1970. An organizational development approach to consulting. *Sloan Management Review*, 12, 51–65.

Mosakowski, E and Earley, P.C. 2000. A selective review of time assumptions in strategy work. *The Academy of Management Review*, 25(4), 796–812.

Reay, T. and Hinings, C.R. 2009. Managing the rivalry of competing institutional logics. *Organization Studies*, 30(6), 629–52.

Sama, A. 2009. The use of history in organizational consultancy interventions, in *Mind-ful Consulting*, edited by S. Whittle and K. Izod. London: Karnac Books, 181–98.

Sandelands, L.E. and Stablein, R.E. 1987. The concept of organization mind, in *Research in the Sociology of Organizations*, edited by S. Bacharach and N. DiTomaso, 5, 135–61.

Schein, E. 1985. *Organizational Culture and Leadership*. San Francisco, CA: Jossey-Bass.

Schein, E. 1998. *Process Consultation Revisited: Building the Helping Relationship*. London: Prentice Hall.

Sinha, C., Sinha, V., Zinken, J. and Sampaio, W. 2006. When time is not space: The social and linguistic construction of time intervals and temporal event relations in an Amazonian culture. Available at: http://www.port.ac.uk/departments/academic/psychology/staff/downloads/filetodownload,121819,en.pdf [accessed: 22 May 2011].

Vimal Ram, L.P. and Davia, C.J. 2010. Phenomenal time and its biological correlates. *Journal of Consciousness Exploration and Research*, 1(5), 560–72.

Weick, K.E. 1989. Theory construction as disciplined imagination. *The Academy of Management Review*, 14(4), 516–31.

Whittle, S. 2009. The challenge of a mind-ful approach to organizational consulting, Introduction to *Mind-ful Consulting*, edited by S. Whittle and K. Izod. London: Karnac Books.

Whittle, S. and Izod, K. (eds.) 2009. *Mind-ful Consulting*. London: Karnac Books.

Wittman, M. 2009. The inner experience of time. *Philosophical Transactions of the Royal Society*, Series B, Biological Sciences, 1955–67. Available at: http://www.biomedexperts.com/Profile.bme/1640663/Marc_Wittmann

6

Family Business: Inside and Outside the Systems at Play

Sally R. Wigutow

Working with Family Business

Several years ago a colleague hired me to work with him in a family business in which the entrepreneur's life stage and her organization's stage of development were not aligned (Gersick et al. 1997). (I have changed the names and details in the stories you'll read about in this chapter.) I was asked to do an organizational role consultation with Elaine, the founder of a summer camp and school she founded in her early fifties as an extension of her original profession as a grade school teacher. She was in her late sixties when we began to work together. My colleague worked with Elaine's eldest son, the COO (Chief Operating Officer), and two other non-family key employees. The business had grown tremendously and now, all these years later, she was tired and wanted to think about pulling back on the one hand but was unable to do so financially on the other.

Survival was still a very real threat in spite of the company's tremendous growth. Having extended her credit too many times to finance that growth, her financial future and legacy rested with her eldest son, although he was not yet ready to take on the overall organizational responsibilities. At her stage of life, this was a difficult position to be in, made more complex as historic family expectations and behaviours were enacted in ways that were often in contradiction to the needs of the organization. My colleague and I found ourselves enmeshed in their dynamics, managing the 'boundaries' (Hayden and Molenkamp 2002) of family and organization – insiders in the organization, outsiders in the family and sometimes the reverse.

For family members and non-family executives and employees, working in a family enterprise can be a blessing and a curse, and usually the experience lies between the ends of this continuum, constantly moving between them. Work takes place within a multi-faceted system imbued with the history of a particular family; it is usually one that holds all the triggers necessary for emotional response on the part of each participant, family and non-family alike.

Within the organization of family business, three systems are alive and active: family, management and governance. There are inevitable tensions because of the overlap of these systems – multiple roles, expectations in one role projected onto another, and assumptions about one system implanted in another. Being able to look at these inherent tensions from the balcony (Heifetz 1994), to see the overlapping systems at play, and to understand their impact on work and family is a large part of an organizational consultation to family owned enterprise. It is as if the consultation creates a holding environment (Winnicott 1986) for the work. It is a challenge to be inside enough to have access to familial dynamics and yet outside enough so as not to enact those same dynamics. The goal is to help the client system develop the capacity to reflect on the tensions between and within the different systems to further enable more thoughtful decision-making. Any task taken up by an internal manager or employee or by an outside organizational consultant, financial or legal advisor in or with a family-managed enterprise is hampered without an appreciation of the many dynamics at play.

The Three Circles

I have found the simple model shown in Figure 6.1, entitled 'The three circles of family business', a very useful one (Tagiuri and Davis 1982). Though it looks simple, it holds great potential for developing an understanding of the inherent complexity embodied in the overlaps of the family, management and ownership circles.

Note the seven possible roles and perspectives. Imagine how differently people perceive the business based on these roles and perspectives and what their expectations are. How there might be intra-personal tensions in addition to inter-personal and inter-group tensions. There might be family members who are owners (5) and don't work in the business and want, perhaps need, the dividends the company generates. They don't necessarily want profit reinvested in the business, and they may not support what they feel is extraordinary compensation for family members who are employees. Next to this are the family members who do work and are owners (7) and may want to reinvest profit. They might think that better-than-fair compensation

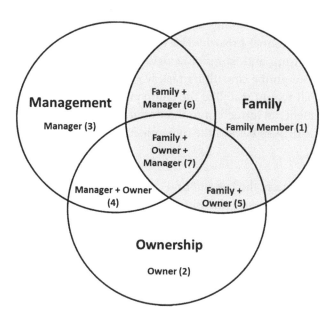

Figure 6.1   The three circles of family business

is their due. Or, how about a family member in management who isn't an owner and consistently maintains hope that they will become an owner (6)? Their experience is filtered through this desire and they can feel they deserve or are perhaps entitled to anything they can take as, after all, they are not the owners they think they should be. Looking at the overlap of the ownership and management circles, you could imagine there might be a non-family key executive with a small ownership stake (4). This person might want to reinvest profit or take a dividend. We don't know but we know for sure they don't want family members taking too much of the compensation pot.

Moving inside and out of these different systems is the context of work with family business. Working to align potentially different agendas is a large part of the task. This chapter holds my stories of practice told in the context of and linked to ways of thinking about the different systems at play. First, I return to Elaine's story.

Elaine's Story and The Systems In Play

Thinking about the family circle and Elaine's life stage, it's logical to think she might pass leadership on to her son but in reality she, her son, and the organization were just learning how to work together to manage the business and to create intentional growth. The organization struggled with the work of being a start-up and simultaneously dealing with formalization and expansion. Although the consulting task was to create organizational systems and policies that would stabilize the company and permit sustained growth, crisis management, an attraction to the dramatic, and the fantasy of a saviour continued to be drivers behind the dynamic interactions of this family and the organization.

In the consultation, the behavioural dynamic that evolved within our team came to parallel the dynamic within the organization. My colleague, Sam, was our team leader. He is younger than I am and consulted to Elaine's son while I worked with Elaine. Initially, this seemed to be a good match: younger son, older man. But in this case, I was an employee, as was her son, and in terms of creating a useful organizational parallel, perhaps her son and I might have been paired to work together, as might have Sam and Elaine. They were each in positions of leadership; each had formal authority and shared the experience of business ownership. Sam and I might have talked about our pairing that paralleled the younger man/older woman pair in the client system. We might have talked about authority and issues of power; we might have talked about what was working and what was not in our consultation and in our relationship so that we could use what we discovered in our work with the client, but we did not. I think we were too far in to see the dynamic we had absorbed. In the end, our lack of conversation was important.

One of the presenting issues was that communication between Elaine and her son was not effective. Elaine's son and Sam held the view that Elaine did not recognize boundaries and that her leadership style was more familial than organizational. She took her authority from the family circle rather than from her role as CEO or owner.

It became clear that Elaine's son was very ambivalent about working with his mother as his boss. We can imagine that his ambivalence is rooted in familial tensions (the family circle). The unclear design of their roles and the lack of a clear authority structure in the company (the management circle) would have exacerbated his ambivalence and made it more difficult to work through. In conversation, Sam told me that Elaine needed to learn about boundaries and that she needed to be contained. He said that Elaine needed to give her son more space to learn to manage – that he could not learn to take his role fully unless I could help her recognize these boundaries. I began to wonder if Sam and Elaine's son were concerned with leadership development alone or might also, and unconsciously, wish that Elaine be extruded from the organization.

Though Sam would probably not agree with my hypothesis, I think it was the latter. He continued to ask for more reports on my 'progress' toward achieving this goal of containment and I increasingly wanted to resist what I experienced as his restraint of me – the feeling I imagine Elaine experienced with her son and he with her. Was this behaviour really an indication of his wish to extrude his mother? I can't know that but as she was the majority owner it would have been impossible. At the time I was not aware that my experience paralleled the client's experience (Bromberg 1982). Unfortunately I could not see that the same situation might be true in my relationship with Sam. It didn't occur to me that I'd be the one to be precipitously removed, and I was.

When I separated from the emotional piece of this experience, the parallel process became apparent. I came to see that Sam and I had enacted a fantasized/ wished for familial and organizational dynamic.

We worked effectively with the rest of the organization (management circle) as they created new business processes and procedures because there were fewer family dynamics in play. But we had been unconsciously pulled inside the family circle and enacted their dynamic.

Inside Family Business Communications

In a family business there is often a private language – verbal shorthand. Sometimes this is great – a raised eyebrow and you've spoken a paragraph! Learning the shorthand brings the consultant inside enough to recognize that real task-oriented communication may be distorted because conversation is replete with assumptions and action is based on presumed understanding without clarification. The language is relational with a family history and is often tolerated beyond its real usefulness to the business of business. Being outside permits the consultant to see this process and bring awareness to the discussions.

David, the eldest, shares ownership of a large ball bearing manufacturing plant and importing firm with his brothers. He is also the best sales person in the entire company. When he tells his partners (his brothers) that he'll be at a trade show to meet potential customers, they know that the show is being held some place where there's golf, because otherwise David won't go. And when one of them is looking for him at the end of the week, someone else is bound to say, 'It's Friday'. Even though Friday is a proper workday, no one expects David to be in. Everyone understands David's behaviour, speaks his language and knows he is indirectly saying that he doesn't really need to care about the norms of the workplace, because he is an owner.

On the other hand, the shorthand can get in the way, actually preventing the family and others in the organization from acknowledging the value that David does contribute … not just the sales themselves but the strategic thinking behind those sales. These familial patterns make it harder for David to take himself seriously, to own and develop further that same strategic thinking. They limit his ability to be fully invested and weaken the expectation that he will be. With enough knowledge of a family's dynamic and clarity about the organizational task, a family business consultant is in the position to help unpack these routines to support personal and organizational growth.

In a second-generation antique store three siblings inherited from their father they sell collectibles, furnishings and art. As the current owners and managers they continued to argue about who works harder and about what is 'fair'. Who took a longer lunch hour, which sibling 'always' got to work with celebrity clients, and who took how many days off are all tallied. None of them thought about what the demands of work might be in the changing context of the marketplace of their industry. Most dialogue took place within the family circle and not in the arena of business management or marketplace need. Helping the siblings to have conversations as business partners and managers as well as siblings was the focus of this consultation.

One objective of this consultation and others like it is to increase a client's ability to recognize these characteristics, both the constructive and disruptive aspects of behaviour, and to help them use this recognition as a source for increased intentionality and strategic choice making. In all organizations, one strategic choice precludes another. In a family business, choices may privilege one 'system' over another. With this client, the task was to help family members differentiate the roles they hold in the company from those they hold in the family. We identify the tasks associated with these roles and help our clients to learn to communicate as family members, sibling to sibling or sibling to parent, or as manager to manager in support of the family and corporate goals. In this way both the family system and management system are respected and strengthened.

Meaning Making

As an organizational insider and family outsider, one recognizes quickly the multiple meanings a business has for a particular family. One client, the son of the founder of a national delivery company, spoke about the great sense of pride he feels when he sees trucks with his family's name on the highway or local street. Sometimes, however, the sense of identity a family feels is so fully fused with that of the company it is difficult for them to think into the future to manage demands of their business environment. Such thinking might require change, which is unimaginable because meaning in a family business is often powerfully linked to the many stories and images of the past as it is in families. Some families in business don't know how to be connected as family members except through the activities of their business. Their relationship as family members is contained within the physical parameters of their workplace, enacted in their management roles.

The siblings who own the antique store have worked together for many decades and have had employees who have worked with them for almost that long. What's inside and what's outside the family, the enterprise? Who is the family? These siblings don't spend social time together. Their relationship with each other takes place within the walls of their shared business and to my mind; it is to the loss of their relationship to each other as individuals, siblings and a family. For them, family exists only in the identity of their shared company and its history. This is the way they understand the concept of family. This behaviour has consequences for both the family and development of the organization, just as acceptance of David's behaviour foreclosed his own development and limited his contribution to the business.

Questions that arise in consulting to these businesses include: So what's important in which system and at what life and organizational stage? How are they different? What needs to be protected and what is being sustained? Certainly it's the viability of the business itself as it is the business that financially supports the family. But it may also be ideas, feelings, community perception, wishes or heartfelt pictures of a family – or the integrity and/or growth of the enterprise itself. What is most important can shift over time. And how does a family business consultant who is an outsider working inside understand and use such an understanding as they take up whatever the consultation task may be? The complex mix of family fantasy/belief, organizational need and marketplace reality is the framework, no piece of which may be ignored. As the insider from the outside, I have the opportunity to present the 'what ifs', the gaps in thinking/logic and emotion, and the questions about what might be gained or lost to which system with what choices. The stated task, whatever it is, transforms into one of raising choice making to a conscious level.

But issues of identity and pride have many benefits in a family business as these are what often sustain the emotional system of the family and the organization. Although issues of family identity and pride may become a constraining force by limiting openness to new ideas and perspectives, they are often also an asset in that people like the experience of buying from, selling to, and working with a family business. And, because it is important to the business-owning family and customers or clients, it is meaningful to employees who may sustain part of their own identity by being part of an organizational culture infused with family stories and myths.

An overarching question becomes clearer – does the family exist for the business or the does the business exist for the family? Issues of role, task, authority and boundaries are all linked to this question. Which of the three circles does the family forefront? And does it happen with consciousness or not? Being inside permits one to look for the underlying thinking and feeling; being outside permits one to engage with the information one discovers by sharing it with the organization and family.

The Dynamic of Multiple Roles

In the ball-bearing company I mentioned earlier, David, the best salesman in the company, brother, and an owner, was angry. He was angry because his sister, the newly named head of the division for which he sold the most material, asked to accompany him on his next sales trip so she could introduce herself to their largest customers. He ignored her request, her emails, phone calls and, guess what? She lost her temper, big time! In terms of the task of the company, of good business practice, hers was a reasonable request, in fact, a strategic one. What else might this be about? Was David enacting his role as oldest brother and just couldn't be bothered with the needs of a younger sister despite her real management role? Was he assuming that, as an owner, he could do as he wished regardless of the company's goals? And how might he have managed the situation had he been able to differentiate the roles and kept the larger primary task (Hirschhorn 1988) in mind?

But David's sister did lose her temper and behaved inappropriately. Did she lose her temper as a sister, with memories of past wrongs in her head and heart? Or, as the division head, angered by a bad decision by a manager? As David is also an owner but his sister is not, what part might this inequality of status play? Being the outsider inside, I suggested that it might be both. I asked each how their response might have been different if they'd been aware of the distinction and been able to address the situation from appropriately parallel roles, sibling to sibling or division head to head of sales. How could they have addressed their own particular needs, in each of their roles, in the appropriate arena?

I became aware of this confusion through my own internal experience of their interaction wanting to speak out to my sense of self-righteousness on her behalf. I felt the push and pull of familiar roles from my family experience, of gender issues and of memories of my own family's business. Being an insider to such experiences and an outsider to this family and organization allowed me the opportunity to make use of my own emotional experience of the situation to help the organization members understand the dynamics they were experiencing.

Family members may have a role in one arena or in all three; it is in the gaps and overlaps that tensions are present. In an earlier consultation to a family-held insurance company, I learned that the family expectation of Susan, the eldest sibling and CEO, was that she would grow the business and at the same time sustain her brother's employment in the company despite his lack of performance. She struggled to manage the tension between being a business leader with a defined goal as well as a sister and daughter with an equally defined goal. For her, a family value predominated. This was the expectation that as a sister, she would take care of her brother. This was part of the story of her childhood. Her competence, industry expertise, and accomplishment did not change the role assigned to her by her family. The role assigned to her by her family affected both how she could take up her role and how she was permitted to take up her role in the business.

Working with family enterprises, I am always an outsider to those who work in the enterprise and to those who are members of the family, or I am an insider to one group and an outsider to the other. Coming into this system, I am often perceived as an ally of any one of many stakeholders, which automatically distances me from others. Each aspect of my personal identity – race, class, age, gender, appearance as well as my presentation of self – pulls me closer or pushes me further away, as does the emotional current I bring with me from my own family of origin. Only when I have been inside long enough to be seen beyond these attributes and long enough to recognize my own responses to the pushes and pulls of this family that resonate with those from my family of origin can I be both inside and outside.

Through time and familiarity I can be inside enough to learn of family secrets – those myths and stories that families don't always want to share with outsiders. Secrets have ongoing repercussions and are often enacted in the course of business in some fashion or another. They pose a problem to good organizational practice in any organization. In a family enterprise, although they may not serve good organizational practice, they often support the homeostasis of the family's emotional system (Friedman 1977). These secrets diminish potential for development by sustaining and hiding the anxiety they generate. Each family has something they think they need to protect from others or indeed hide from themselves.

The siblings who own the antique store are also owners of a large block of real estate. The real estate is of far greater worth than the store; it is a more financially successful 'business' but talking about it as such would bring them into a discussion of ownership, which in turn would open up topics they do not wish to discuss. Instead, the siblings talk about the everydayness of business in the store because this is what represents and sustains their picture of family. When I brought up the disposition of ownership and asked them how they envisioned the future, my question was buried and the conversation was redirected quickly to operational issues. The siblings could have created and supported any permutation of third-generation ownership through thoughtful planning. However, because it's been a 'secret', though known, that one sibling favours some children more than others, it is feared that should this sentiment be discussed openly, the family relationship would be threatened and such a rupture could not be risked. Who liked who more became too difficult a conversation and the family managed this tension about future ownership by remaining stuck in the worries of daily operations.

In my role, I am an outsider and I can never know at the outset what picture a family holds of its relation to the enterprise or what dynamics are being played out within and between the family, ownership and management systems. A family often doesn't see or hold a picture either but acts nevertheless as if there is one. I often feel as if I'm in a complex dance moving between systems, with more access to one, less to another since families don't usually share the information a consultant thinks necessary. The dance involves balancing the inside and outside experience: first to unpack the elements of each system well enough to grasp who is involved and what the moving pieces are and then to understand how they either restrain or complement each other. It is a slow dance working to understand what value/s might underlie behaviour and choice-making in each system, how they are linked and what is actually possible around issues of organizational change. One of the tasks, and sometimes it is the primary one, is to hold the insider/outsider role well enough to be a container to permit recognition, learning and intentional choice-making to evolve.

Conclusion

The three-circle model presented earlier is a useful analytic tool. It has helped me understand and navigate the dynamics of the multiple systems at play. It provokes questions about roles, task, boundaries and authority: What role is being enacted when? What tasks are appropriate to the stated role? From which arena do actions derive their authority? What are the perceived and appropriate role and task boundaries? Are roles changing as the organization grows and develops? Do they need to? Most simply: What is going on here and from which system?

I see my role as helping clients gain a better understanding of how the three systems are interdependent and impact each other. The wellbeing of individuals in the family and in the enterprise, of the family as a whole, and of the organization as a business is both supported and challenged by the degree of clarity that can be brought to the systems' overlaps and gaps and to the tensions between them. Simultaneously holding an insider and outsider perspective is a vital piece of this work.

References

Alderfer, C. 1987. An intergroup perspective on group dynamics, in *Handbook of Organizational Behavior*, edited by J.W. Lorsch. Englewood Cliffs, NJ: Prentice-Hall, 190–222.

Friedman, E.H. 1977. Secrets and systems, in *A Collection of Selected Papers*, edited by J. Lorie and L. McClenathan. Washington, DC: Georgetown Family Centre, 61–70.

Gersick, K.E., Davis, J.A., McCollom Hampton, M. and Lansberg, I. 1997. *Generation to Generation: Life Cycles of the Family Business*. Boston, MA: Harvard Business School Press.

Hayden, C. and Molenkamp, R. J. 2002. *Tavistock Primer* II. Jupiter, FL: The A.K. Rice Institute for the Study of Social Systems.

Heifetz, R.A. 1994. *Leadership Without Easy Answers*. Boston, MA: Harvard University Press.

Marris, P. 1974. *Loss and Change*. New York: Pantheon Books.

Tagiuri, R. and Davis, J.A. 1982. Bivalent attributes of the family firm. Working Paper, Harvard Business School, Cambridge, MA. Reprinted 1996, *Family Business Review*, IX (2), 199–208.

Winnicott, D.W. (compiled and edited by C. Winnicott, R. Shepherd and M. Davis) 1986. *Home is Where We Start From: Essays by a Psychoanalyst*. New York and London: W.W. Norton & Company.

7

By Invitation Only?

Lisa Gardiner, Elizabeth Summers and Gerhard Raftl

The decision to work as a relational consultancy provides valuable opportunities to truly connect with our clients and positively influence our practice in organizations. We see this working in two ways. First, in the laws of physics, the position and other properties of objects are only meaningful in relation to other objects. Second, the relationships that we deem successful are characterized by depth and longevity. This enables both client and consultant to craft changes in capacity, built through positive and negative reciprocal actions.

A relational approach requires the organization to invite you in and let you see areas of vulnerability. This experience can create a sense of relief, discomfort, and, at times a hostile dependency. The success of this 'insider' approach relies on building a trusting relationship, being flexible and adaptive and maintaining equilibrium. Responsibility for this aspect often rests with the consultant.

As Senior Consultants at SAL Consulting we, Liz, Gerhard and I, not only work with organizations in a combination of clinical, organizational and professional development roles but we also supervise consultants. We see ourselves at times as insiders through the long-term relationships we have had with multiple organizations over the life of our consultancy.

In this chapter we describe how our relationship with one organization commenced and evolved and some of the challenges associated with this relationship. We also look at how we use a 'thinking and planning' approach that helps to keep us thoughtful within the consultant-client relationship: the Organizational Cultural Assessment and Profile (OCAP).

We explore how positioning consultant/s physically inside the client organization and pairing consultants with identified positions and roles within organizations to develop longitudinal relationships can assist with facilitating change. As with any relationship, there can be ups and downs and the strength of the relationship can be tested. This chapter highlights how we fared in a relationship that took us beyond a simple invitation.

Who Are We?

SAL Consulting, based in Sydney, Australia, started out seven years ago. As an organization we are very aware that we are growing and evolving. Unless we continue to be mindful of the things that matter most, we could lose what makes us 'who we are' and our agreed purpose. In the human services sector, our clients struggle with clarity regarding both identity and purpose and these are the areas of concern where we are asked to provide assistance.

Originally a clinically focused consultancy, we have extended our activities to provide services in organizational development and professional development. We are engaged in work across four states of Australia, primarily on the Eastern Coast. Our clients are government departments, non-government organizations and individuals in the human services sector and, to a lesser degree, education. We have a trans-disciplinary team with key focus areas in therapy, clinical support, training, clinical supervision, education and professional development, operational support and organizational development.

The organizations that engage us work across a range of client groups. However, we are sought out primarily by those organizations that work with very vulnerable populations such as children in care, children and adults with disabilities or autism, children and adults with mental health issues or a history of complex trauma. Often, these individuals are considered to be 'difficult to deal with' and put into the 'too hard' basket for many service providers in this sector.

We find that organizations that approach us for one piece of work, such as an assessment of their clients, or training or a strategic plan, will continue to engage us for at least two years, but more often an engagement will be around five years. This continued engagement provides opportunities for SAL, and the organizations we work with, to take an integrated and multipronged approach to service improvement, staff and organizational development.

In 2012, we have 25 staff and we still maintain the values we started with. We take these values into each piece of work that we do. Our values underpin our ethos and are what we do – dignity, empathy, truthfulness, integrity, responsibility, reward, wisdom, creativity and loyalty. Originally, the ethos statement was created in reaction to what we didn't want to be. Gradually, through our planning meetings and retreats, it evolved to what it is today. Because 'Realized change does not have the same significance independent of how it is achieved' we endorse the view that 'the practice of organizational change should be based on values' (Klev and Levin 2012: 31).

It is important that we continue to incorporate these values consistently. Examples of how our values inform our practice are shown in Table 7.1.

Table 7.1   Excerpts from SAL consulting ethos and values statement

Value	Principles	Practice
Dignity	Cooperation Respect Responsivity Reciprocity	We will consult, talk, listen, ask, suggest, with acceptance We will engage with others to engender respect We will take the time required to reach an agreement
Integrity	Ethics Acting truthfully Inclusive	We will say what we think/believe truthfully We will say no to things we do not feel we can contribute to satisfactorily We will be professional in all dealings We will seek to identify workable options
Reward	Satisfaction Passion	We will strive for personal fulfilment in the work we do We will have fun We will do things that ignite our passion
Creativity	Seeking alternatives Innovation Originality Invention Vision	We will ensure we schedule time to think and reflect We will maintain a balance to ensure that we have the space and the opportunities to be creative We will support others' creativity We will support people to take risks

As we embedded our values into our day-to-day working life, we developed a decision making process, shown in Table 7.2. The decision making process was developed as a result of a discussion held in SAL about the sort of work we wanted to do. We found that with the growth and need for better practice due to a sweep of new agency accreditations in this sector, we were receiving many more requests for our services and were increasingly challenged by our felt need to contribute to sector development. This created a tension between running a consultancy based on market demand and a consultancy that targeted agencies which we felt we could really make a difference for their clients but that could potentially get lost in the turbulence of rapid sector growth.

Table 7.2   SAL Consulting decision making framework

Key Questions	Thinking Guide
1. How will it make a difference?	Will it change something for the better? Can it influence policy or process?
2. How well can we deliver?	Do we have the skills to do a good job? How will it be managed?
3. How can this be an opportunity for collaboration and relationship building?	Can we build on existing relationships? Is this an opportunity to work with someone we don't usually work with?
4. How much passion and drive do we have around this?	Who is excited about this? Does it fit with our strategic direction?
5. How do we retain the vibe?	How can we leave our own mark? How could this potentially change us?
6. What are the potential snakes?	What are the possible risks? What would make things difficult?
7. How will it impact on existing relationships?	Who will care that we do this? Is it an opportunity for strengthening relationships?
8. What are the financial implications?	Does it help us be sustainable? Is it financially viable or a planned loss?
9. How does it impact on our reputation?	What are other people's views about this? Is it something we can proudly put our badge on?

Being a relational consultancy, means we walk alongside our clients, we take an active interest in their development and we develop long-term relationships with organizations. We adapt our services, and at times our own organization, as the client organizations we are working with progress and mature. This can contribute to our own organizational flux and redesign, something we already experience by virtue of being a young organization. Writing this chapter has provided us with a deeper understanding and appreciation of our own presence and identity[1] when working with our client organizations.

Our Context

Over the last 10 years, Australia has experienced growth in multiple sectors and did not experience the Global Financial Crisis to the same extent as other western countries (Australia Unlimited 2011). There has been a focus on social inclusion and providing government funding to those with most need. Whilst

---

1   Presence and Identity is the name of an experiential lab conducted by Dr Susan Whittle and Karen Izod

these initiatives were at a national level, the political and financial climate can vary from state to state.

In New South Wales (NSW), the most populace state, there has been a growing demand for services in the health and human services sector and especially in Out of Home Care and disability areas. Government funding provided to non-government organizations has meant that there has been extreme growth in some organizations and this growth has often occurred before the foundations for good practice were laid. This created an opportunity for consultancies such as ours to respond to some of the sector's need for external assistance to cope with unwieldy and unplanned growth. At the same time, NSW is financially depleted so models of service can be driven by economics rather than quality.

These contextual factors sit alongside the challenges faced by these complex service organizations: how to adapt behaviour to fit the ecology or environment in which they are situated. Organizations, like individuals, develop different strengths and internal resources, depending on experiences. These experiences determine levels of vulnerability and tolerance to adverse situations and shape our sense of optimism or pessimism (Bowlby 1980).

We find that organizations working in the health and human services sector can appear to take on their clients' characteristics and qualities. This isomorphic (being of identical or similar form, shape, or structure to that prevailing in the environment) or parallel processing (where one system has an impact on another) is natural (Davies 1997). If there is some awareness that this process is happening, this can become a positive experience and help organization leaders put in place ways of managing the more restrictive or destructive characteristics and qualities. When there is a lack of awareness of isomorphic processing, we see client characteristics enacted unknowingly by staff and management or embodied unconsciously in strategy, systems and structures. Consequently, this lack of awareness can create problems and internal conflict. We find that the organizational characteristics most often compromised are identity and purpose. Furthermore, those working closely with unaware organizations can also be at risk of parallel processing so relational consultants such as ourselves need to be observant of our own behaviour and interactions. One way we have managed this is through internal professional development where we identify what we have 'picked up' from a client and what that looks like when brought back into our organization.

For example, Organization X commences services as a small disability drop-in support provider with a focus on skills development and quality individual support. Over time, pressures to access funding lead the organization to take on various service models and funding streams and different types of clients, i.e., children and people with mental health support needs. The organization now struggles with engaging skilled and competent staff, and how to provide quality services to a range of different people. They begin to ask … what is our core business? What is our vision? How do we describe ourselves?

These issues of identity and purpose are also common concerns for our most vulnerable populations. All organizations are susceptible to different degrees of compromise, regardless of the field they work in, but the human services sector appears to demonstrate a strong correlation between the level of client vulnerability and the incidences of isomorphism. Recognizing how we, as consultants, unconsciously identify with and reproduce aspects of our client organizations also helps us to work on and address these isomorphic dynamics. In addition, this is where we are able to walk with the client and create a shared awareness of this processing and its impact. Many organizations find they become much more proactive in their own management after becoming aware and gaining an understanding of this particular dynamic.

The following case study provides an opportunity to explore one such organization. City Care has experienced swift growth and significant challenges adapting to their environment. Our contact with the organization also developed and changed rapidly, as we helped them to identify, explore and manage challenges associated their own rapid growth and internal change.

Case Study – Introduction

City Care is a large agency that provides services to people with complex needs. Service recipients include children and young people with developmental experiences of neglect, trauma and/or abuse, people with intellectual disability, challenging behaviour, mental health/psychiatric/autistic spectrum diagnoses or a combination of such presentations.

In this organization there is a 'disconnect' between senior managers and the CEO. The CEO was concerned that the organization reflected good practice but without in depth knowledge of how this might be achieved. She believed that staff (particularly service managers) are 'solely' responsible for service standards, irrespective of structures or principles, and she was focused on growth as a primary objective. The current climate made growth very easy as organizations were rewarded if services could be offered that undercut others financially and if organizations were able to start up service delivery within very short timeframes.

Members of the senior management team were concerned that their infrastructure was inadequate and that City Care reflected an under-informed perspective around good practice and a lack of true focus on person-centredness. This would be the same as a retail customer services manager in a business believing that the business cared about the customers but did not practice in a manner that demonstrated it. At City Care there was a disconnect between the sector's expectations of service standards, the organization's stated aims and the actual practices within many of City Care's service outlets. The glossy brochures describing the organization's vision and range of services available was in stark contrast to the observable practices on the ground.

In addition, City Care lacked sufficient understanding of why clinical support was required and the function or purpose it served, as sub-contractors usually provided expertise in this area. City Care also struggled with the evolution of a workplace culture that appeared to have enabled secretive and self-interested practices to take hold. These included practices driven by staff preference rather than client need, un-approved use of restrictive practices, unreliable implementation of client plans and programs and inaccurate or non-reporting of incidents. Some of these aspects of City Care organization only became apparent as we began to work more closely with them.

CITY CARE PHASE 1: STEPPING OVER THE THRESHOLD

City Care offers psychiatric and behavioural services in both metropolitan and rural regions. The organization operates services across a range of funding programs and employs in excess of 2000 people nationally. They have been established for 15 years.

We were approached initially to provide clinical support to teams who provide services in residential settings across the state of NSW. We discovered that City Care had been working with consultants that they considered were not providing a quality clinical service. Our initial contact, Jim, City Care business development manager, was keen to engage us in a broader manner across the organization but needed to demonstrate that we could deliver a quality service, particularly with City Care's previous experience of hiring consultants. Our initial invitation was to provide clinical services to help City Care staffs:

1.   support children and young people in Out of Home Care; and

2.   address challenging and high-risk behaviour to a small group of City Care clients.

In the beginning, our understanding of the organization's capacity was patchy, primarily communicated to us through Jim, who did not have a thorough operational perspective on how things were working. We had some idea about how City Care managed their relationships with funders and also with the government agencies that managed quality, performance and accreditation. Our growing awareness and concerns around exactly how City Care would provide support for their clients and staff during this growth phase meant that we decided to embark on a six-month relationship with caution, with a firm belief that we would review our involvement carefully following this initial engagement.

In this initial stage, we continued to build the relationship with City Care and in particular through lots of contact with our key contact, Jim. We progressed to a dialogue that was both more comprehensive and deeper in complexity, regarding risk, opportunities for service development and a review of operational issues that were impacting on quality of care. Our work quickly grew to include senior clinical supervision, strategic input into operational issues, multiple clinical supports for staff and clients, and some therapeutic services for individual clients. As City Care expanded across the country, we were also engaged to provide services for them in other parts of the country.

There were three primary reasons why our contract expanded so quickly:

1.   growth in the sector meant that they needed to establish services quickly on the ground to demonstrate to the funder that they were capable of managing the services for which they had tendered;

2.   we were able to demonstrate levels of engagement with staff and efficacy in how our services were provided;

3.   emerging risks and challenges surrounding the provision of services to more complex clients meant there was a greater demand for clinical services.

This time was challenging for us, with many observable risks and practice challenges occurring on a day-to-day basis, as reported back in supervision by our consultants. We relayed our concerns via our key client contacts. But whilst the engagement was still strong and our dialogue with City Care continued, we felt we were able to assist them build capacity through focused clinical support and tailored training.

At this time, the organization restructured their senior management team. Moving (partially promoting and sidelining) Jim into a position far removed from operations, City Care employed Simon, a senior manager with previous experience in government. In retrospect, this was the exact point in time where our relationship with our client changed. Previously arranged work plans were altered, communication became strained (apparently due to some cross-purposes) and our future involvement was beginning to be questioned. It was evident that the previously shared understanding, perspective and approaches to the work were now uncertain and perhaps bordering on absent.

CITY CARE PHASE 2: DOES THE INVITATION STILL STAND?

The transition from Phase 1 to Phase 2 was marked by further management changes and re-structuring. This has been a constant feature of this organization's lifecycle. On this occasion, the changes including re-positioning middle managers into non-direct service roles and a focus on 'cleaning up' poor staff conduct and performance. This led to dramatic changes in practices at a unit level and in how clinical support was being engaged and utilized within the organization. The client's focus was shifting from the progressive development of integrated practice to issue- or incident-management, with a high level of reactivity. From a relational perspective, the notions of 'working together' with collaborative attitudes were disappearing. It became apparent that new limits and boundaries on communication and engagement were becoming set.

Simon, the new Senior Manager and our main contact, made it clear from the outset that his intention was to grow the in-house provision of clinical services. In itself, this was not a concern for us. In many other contracts, we work collaboratively with a client organization's internal clinical teams. However, Simon's desire to grow internal clinical services was influenced heavily by his desire to demonstrate costs savings to the CEO, a limited understanding of the value of clinical services, and a desire to control the way clinical services guided or provided recommendations around risk, service growth and other factors that were connected to operational decision-making. This move to in-house provision saw a disengagement from the clinical guidance and support we provided and, we felt, hindered the development of clinically informed practice. In addition, a number of significant poor planning and service delivery events took place, where services were initiated without appropriate clinical consultation and work increasingly evolved into reactive risk management. During Phase 2, Simon and other middle managers of City Care focused strongly on performance management. Many staff linked with practice concerns were either fired or placed under severe supervisory scrutiny until they left City Care. The somewhat zealous and under-developed approach that was taken resulted in further staff attrition.

It was during this time that we suggested that an alternative way of improving performance and developing staff more effectively was to provide directed training and support that would help learning transfer back into the workplace. A leadership development program was initiated. This included a clinical framework and individual development, utilizing teaming and questioning approaches. In the implementation of this program, a range of cultural and capacity issues in several service teams was highlighted and the discord within and between middle management and unit management ranks became more apparent. Despite these issues, the program was taken up very well by many of the participants, however not by Simon, who appeared to take an even stronger adversarial position to moving forward in a positive frame. Figure 7.1 shows the presence of SAL consultants in City Care during Phase 2.

Our relationship with City Care became increasingly difficult to manage. From our clinical knowledge, it was clear to us that City Care was at risk in a number of ways, but our attempts to increase the dialogue between our organizations to assist City Care to better manage the risks failed. Despite what we perceived as an increased need for clinical and planning supports, both on the ground and with middle management, and opportunities for embedding a new type of thinking following the customized leadership training, Simon introduced changes that resulted in significant reductions in the provision of clinical services offered by City Care and reductions in the service we were providing.

Our involvement had now changed from multiple connection points with the organization, focusing on practice-building, to only providing services:

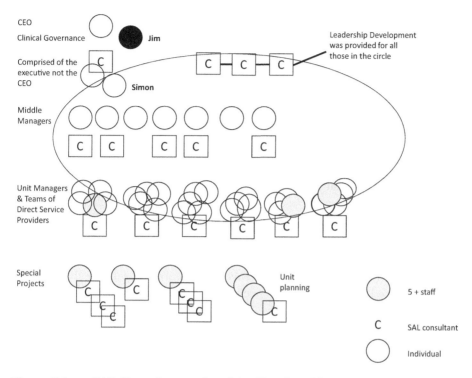

Figure 7.1   SAL Consultants placed in City Care Phase 2

1. where the organization was under scrutiny from the funder, in relation to quality of service; or

2. where City Care perceived there was a high risk of service failure.

The organizational issues impacted significantly on the services that City Care clients received. Effectively, our involvement had changed from an open invitation to a selective invitation around particular issues. Despite our conditional involvement, which was becoming increasingly hampered by decreasing levels of engagement and caveats around how and what information was provided to us, the organization continued to champion the 'clinical partnership' between SAL and City Care to the funding bodies they were desperately attempting to please.

Our broad thinking at this time was to try to influence City Care staff by placing and replacing our consultants in positions when they could model positive and client-centred behaviour with those staff that we felt were most able to change. While we had some influence at middle management and at a direct service level, we had the least linkage and influence in the executive structure (see Figure 7.1).

In his research into residential services for young people in out-of-home care placements, James Anglin identified one core theme – congruence in service of children's best interests. He described that a 'service unit' may demonstrate congruence or incongruence to varying degrees across its elements, processes and overall operation. He describes each service unit and an agency as a whole to be engaged in what he termed a 'struggle for congruence' (Anglin 2002, Anglin 2003).

This notion of congruence with children's best interests readily equates to a term now in common use in NSW, 'person-centred' practice. In respect of City Care, the view of SAL Consultants was that progress toward both authentic 'person-centredness' and 'congruence in service' was stalled and at risk.

At SAL, we also came to recognize the effect on our staff and our thinking as we grew more concerned and frustrated, while remaining hopeful that opportunity for improved engagement might be forthcoming. We realize this was a 'Pollyanna' or optimist's perspective of sorts. Our key consultants became polarized in their views about how to approach the loss of connectivity, communication and efficacy in our relationship with City Care. This division in part related to views about the best route to remediate the issues and potential for splintering of existing connections. Those most closely involved in direct delivery thought that some promise remained within middle management and in pockets of staff at the direct-service level.

At this point, we reviewed the Organizational Cultural Assessment and Profile (OCAP) we had created of City Care. The OCAP assists SAL consultants in holding relationships in ways that are helpful to the client. An OCAP meeting brings together the conductor (the SAL consultant responsible for managing our relationship with the client organization and for project management) and all the consultants that currently, or expect to be, working with the client organization. The number of consultants in the meeting depends on how many SAL consultants are working in the organization. For larger organizations, there are usually seven or so consultants. With City Care there were 13.

A SAL consultant who is not closely involved with the client organization facilitates the meeting. The facilitating consultant listens and asks questions that draw out experiences and examples that can highlight barriers or pathways to achieving success. Each consultant talks about the work they are doing and how they are working with people in their area of the client organization. Consultants and the conductor ask questions of each other. Any problems or concerns that have not been picked up in practice supervision are then taken back to supervision. Such issues are also subsequently raised with the client organization by the conductor and worked through together. This process ripples through each consultant and the internal staff member or members with whom they have a relationship. We run a series of OCAP meetings over a client's project life cycle. The initial OCAP relies on a combination of known fact, predictive work and the quality of relationships between the organization and our consultancy. The OCAP works by balancing guiding questions with the process of gathering our consultants together to offer inputs to process. This helps us to reflect, exchange perspectives, look at the current situations and plan for the future. It is a process that happens on a regular basis and develops our knowledge and understanding of the client organization. It is especially helpful when we encounter stumbling blocks. OCAP meetings, together with supervision and regular contact with the contract conductor, create a web of relational data and support for our consultants.

At this particular point in time in our contract with City Care, the review of the City Care OCAP took many hours to complete and required a high level of input and analysis from all the consultants involved. Following this review process (on another day!) we moved onto completing the Organizational Relationship Assessment Tool (ORAT). ORAT has been developed to assist SAL consultants:

1.   to reflect on a set of identified characteristics that in our experience appear to correlate to clients' 'readiness' and ' non-readiness' for support; and

2.   to provide client organizations with a self-appraisal tool to monitor that readiness.

We do this by assessing the quality of engagement. The ORAT is another data thread informing our web of support and is designed to periodically gauge and quantify the strength and quality of client engagement during SAL Consulting's involvement along 12 dimensions. These are shown in Table 7.3 on the following page.

Table 7.3   ORAT (Organizational Relational Assessment Tool) dimensions

+ve Characteristics (Promoting relational engagement and indicative of 'readiness' for support)	Relational Diagnostic Clusters	-ve Characteristics (Inhibiting relational engagement and indicative of 'non-readiness' for support)
Assertiveness		Hostility
Willing/Open	Connectedness	Resistant
Engaged		Avoidant
Inter-dependent		Dependency
Flexibility	State	Locked Down
In Motion/Evolving		Inert
Informed/Aware		Blinkered/Oblivious
Organized/Ordered	Affect	Disorganized/Disordered
Optimistic		Pessimistic
Mindful/Calm		Chaotic/Frantic
Risk Considerate	Presence	Gambler
Courageous		Risk Averse

We assess readiness for acceptance of support by posing a series of questions about the relational behaviour of each of the individuals and groupings of people we are working with or having some contact with prior to and during the consultation. Depending on the level of organizational congruency and cohesion, the organization may generally demonstrate more positive or more negative characteristics. However, the organization may demonstrate a split, showing both positive and negative characteristics but in differing areas of the organization, or positive and negative characteristics may be held throughout the organization.

To illustrate a split between positive and negative: a CEO contacts our consultancy to request we work with multiple staff teams to develop improved practice. The CEO may be willing and optimistic but many staff members may be hostile and resistant, already believing that they provide excellent care to their clients and therefore training, clinical development and support is seen as a waste of time. Where positive and negative characteristics are held throughout the organization, we can experience a sense of organizational ambivalence that can demonstrate itself in different ways, for example there maybe initial engagement but it may be weak resulting in lack of follow through, missed appointments, lack of organized attendance at training days, etc. The ORAT process assists us in planning the strategies of engagement and provides the foundation for planning, monitoring and communicating small changes when they occur with multiple consultants. Table 7.4 shows a précis excerpt from the Organizational

Table 7.4   ORAT appraisal for City Care Phase 2

+ve Characteristics (Promoting relational engagement and indicative of 'readiness' for support)	Relational Diagnostic Clusters	-ve Characteristics (Inhibiting relational engagement and indicative of 'non-readiness' for support)
	Connectedness	Hostility
		Resistant
		Avoidant
	State	Dependency
		Locked Down
		Inert
	Affect	Blinkered/Oblivious
		Disorganized/Disordered
		Pessimistic
	Presence	Chaotic/Frantic
		Gambler
Courageous		

Relational Assessment Tool (ORAT), summarizing the appraisal of engagement and receptiveness in Phase 2 of our involvement with some City Care managers.

Not only is the ORAT an important tool for assessing an organization's engagement, it is also a helpful reflective tool. It helps our organization to assess the impact on SAL of engaging with our clients. By reflecting on ourselves during a client contract and thinking about how we may be demonstrating particular characteristics (both positive and negative manifestations), we find we can to make an enormous difference both to the engagement of the client organization in its own development and the development of our consultants.

Following our ORAT analysis and our reflection on the relationship between our organizations, our involvement with City Care now shifted to focus on:

1. completion of existing project work associated with establishment of a new service in another jurisdiction; and
2. bridging some gaps while the new in-house clinical services were effectively constituted.

This had been delayed as staff turnover continued at direct service, unit management and middle management levels. Our involvement appeared to be that of holding (Winnicott 1965) City Care in some key service areas, particularly where the funder's scrutiny was acute and senior management within City Care were particularly anxious regarding scrutiny. This sense of being held offers the client a facilitating environment (Winnicott 1965). The supportive facilitation provides a sense of scaffolding, and a type of organizational co-regulation that in turn establishes a platform to move forward. This enables us to:

- Assess the challenges that our client organizations face both internally and through their interface with the service sector.

- Consider the types of clients they are delivering a service to, the level of complexity and challenge these clients provide, and the position, skill level, experience, and specific support needs or challenges that the individuals served by the organization may have.

- Better understand the way each organization operates by focusing on aspects such as their strengths, weaknesses, key personnel, team and organizational idiosyncrasies and culture

- Match our consultants with the people identified in key positions, or roles, within the client organization.

Responsibility for holding the relationship, while encouraging mutual respect and accountability, sits with the consultant. In any consulting relationship the challenge is to develop and maintain boundaries, trust, and to continue to move forward, often in difficult circumstances. A typical challenge is how familiarity can create discomfort in providing feedback or offering an objective perspective to a client.

CITY CARE PHASE 3: SHOULD WE STAY OR SHOULD WE GO? THE DILEMMA ASSOCIATED WITH THE CERTAINTY OF CHANGE

Throughout the latter period of Phase 2, we had been reviewing and considering the value and usefulness of our ongoing involvement with City Care. Phase 3 was marked by another significant management restructure that brought a couple of experienced operational managers into the agency. These new staff members brought a willingness to engage and evaluate previous initiatives. Our connection with City Care was restructured, and we now connected with these new people rather than Simon.

At SAL Consulting we experience change almost every single day. While it can be very disconcerting and unhelpful in many circumstances, the opposite can also be true. The staffing re-structure certainly yielded increased potential and with it came an opportunity to re-frame the engagement from a holding relationship where negative characteristics prevailed (i.e. those inhibiting relational engagement and indicative of 'non-readiness' for support) to 'pressing' the relationship, where City Care might accept an increased share both collaborative working and progressing forward with agreed tasks and initiatives.

Therefore, during Phase 3, we made the decision to complete the existing contract arrangements and finish things off. This decision created a reaction with the new operational people, who were reluctant for us to discontinue services and approached us to re-engage. We hoped this was a signal that City Care was evolving a shared and better understanding of the functions of clinical supports, the role of leadership and the benefits of effective management systems. More likely, however, was the reality that these new managers had developed a relationship with us that was unaffected by the tensions and challenges that characterized our work with Simon. Their experience was that of positive, effective support. A challenge for us in this situation was to allow this relationship with them to develop unhindered by our own previous experiences. We noticed that recruitment of these new operational managers had led to an improved understanding of our previous interventions and appreciation of some of our initiatives, such as our work with strategic organizational planning and design at a unit level (see Figure 7.1). Our improved working relationship is reflected in the evolving ORAT profile shown in Table 7.5.

Table 7.5   City Care ORAT Profile – management level end of Phase 3

+ve Characteristics (Promoting relational engagement and indicative of 'readiness' for support)	Relational Diagnostic Clusters	-ve Characteristics (Inhibiting relational engagement and indicative of 'non-readiness' for support)
Assertiveness		
Willing/Open	Connectedness	
Engaged		
		Dependency
	State	
In Motion/Evolving		Inert
Informed/Aware		Blinkered/Oblivious
Organized/Ordered	Affect	Disorganized/Disordered
		Pessimistic
		Chaotic/Frantic
	Presence	Gambler
Courageous		

Table 7.6   SAL Consulting's work with City Care Phases 1–3

	Phase 1	Phase 2	Phase 3
Our invitation	Clinical Services	Clinical advice and support Supervision of staff Training Therapy Mediation	Clinical Services
Our role(s)	Senior Practitioner Clinicians	Senior Practitioner Clinicians Supervisor clinical Supervisor management Trainers/facilitators Therapist Mediator	Senior Practitioner Clinician
Our tasks	Clinical advice Clinical support Practice enhancement	Clinical advice Clinical support Practice enhancement Training Professional development and practice enhancement Therapy for clients of City Care Mediation between new service director and staff from existing service from take over	Clinical advice Clinical support Practice enhancement
What helped us work on the task	Initial planning, mapping and matching process Time to consider what we thought was the best strategy Government pressure on CC to provide a better service	Meeting when we could communicate what the achievements were Initial OCAP Increased supervision for consultants working with teams Increased focus on clinical professional development at City Care and our consultancy	More defined area of work Smaller group of consultants Change of staff leading to an increase in receptiveness in City Care at middle manager level Finishing the contract

Table 7.6   Continued

	Phase 1	Phase 2	Phase 3
What hindered our work	Not enough access into CC to demonstrate good practice Change of personnel at CC Lack of understanding at the executive level about leadership, good practice and staff support	Three different people holding the contract Lack of time to communicate Divergent views between our consultancy and City Care Divergent views internally in our consultancy Patchy communication City Care staff deriving benefit from the organisational dysfunction Difficulty following our own processes	Communication was still at times patchy The good work was recognised only in pockets City Care underwent further structural change
What happened	Practice improved in an ad hoc way Increase in divergent views about how CC should function	Projects work yielded good results Individual supervision strengthen individual practice The support our consultancy appeared to provide City Care with more confidence to grow as opposed to a focus on consolidation	Initially, holding CC in key areas of vulnerability only. Over time in this phase and through renewed connectedness of new key operational managers, CC began to consider their need to build a practice framework and make investment in building clinical services Previous SAL work and approaches more broadly recognized and increasing requests for services Renewal of previously introduced initiatives

Over time, our involvement began to expand in some target areas and the climate for our involvement was shifting. New personnel contributed to better connections with us in a range of ways, including some re-framing of perceptions around readiness for engagement and support. Our work in phases 1–3 is shown in Table 7.6.

CITY CARE PHASE FOUR: ACCEPTING A NEW INVITATION – ON OUR TERMS?

We stepped into Phase 4 through the negotiation of a new contract and looked to the future with anticipation, caution and some optimism. Our optimism was derived from an executive level commitment to establish a clinical practice framework across City Care, as well as a re-exploration and reprise of the leadership and performance management initiatives. SAL Consulting has been invited in to assist in the development of this framework – allowing us to revisit the discussions, information and scope of our involvement with City Care from several years ago. We had known that this invitation was 'in the post', but we were unsure that we wanted to open it.

We have moved forward into phase 4 and so far it has been working well. We have learnt many lessons through our experiences in phases 1–3. In some ways our learning has seemed in parallel to the learning that has occurred in City Care. Deciding to finish the contract at a time of our choosing presented us with a new opportunity to discuss the impact that City Care had had on our own consultancy, in both positive and negative ways. The relationship had taken us places that we were not fully prepared to go but had helped us to strengthen our consultancy. It showed us the weaknesses and the gaps in our approach. We reflected heavily on how the depth of relationship necessary for the work we were undertaking with City Care also placed us at greater risk of isomorphism. This reflective process also allowed us to start a new contract with far more defined and realistic parameters and a simultaneously more rigorous and iterative approach.

City Care: What Happened at SAL Consulting

With exception of the first two OCAPs, the processes surrounding our engagement with City Care seemed to never work in the usual way. We had so many SAL Consulting people working in the client organization that a 'neutral' facilitator for our OCAP and ORAT meetings was difficult to find. We allowed the role of conductor (managing our contract with City Care) to become unclear, and at times, there were three people in this role. Consequently, just finding time to attend the scheduled meetings and ensuring we had a congruent perspective and shared understandings became almost impossible. Due to the level of effort required to work in a risk-laden environment and the emotional drain on our consultants when constantly engaging with negative or resistant City Care staff, we found that the processes we had put in place were not always followed by our consultants, and at times, our way of working began to mirror City Care's.

Our perspectives and our ability to effectively communicate in our own organization started to fracture as we tried to find a way forward. Our consultants had different views about how to hold City Care and how we should be managing our contract with them. Divergent views are usually seen as a positive sign for our consultancy, but this time they seemed to create disagreement and discord instead of a way forward. We noticed that numerous decisions were made that no longer followed our decision-making process (see Table 7.2 for SAL decision-making process).

When we were related to as insiders, the cultural characteristics were that of a dysfunctional family, brimming with all of the factions, folklore and frustrations that can become self-reinforcing. Some of our consultants started to overly identify with those who they felt were helpless or hopeless in the client organization. The ORAC and ORAT processes were developed to provide specific responses to the problem of SAL consultants 'being too far in'. At these times we found internal supervision alone was inadequate to support our consultants' boundary management needs. In response to these challenges, we decided to increase our internal planning and support processes, including:

- Trying to regain some understanding about our strategic direction with this client (this did not work well).

- Debriefing of our staff.

- Additional supervision.

Our involvement with City Care demonstrated to us, that despite all our analysis and planning processes, at times we are also at risk of being drawn into our client's organizational politics or vulnerability dynamic. At SAL Consulting we call that being pulled 'into the box', where the consultant cannot manage effective boundaries. This means consultants have decreased capacity to provide a secure base for their clients (Raftl 2001; Bowlby 1980; Hughes 1997; Crittenden 2006). If we had been more aware that we had become more like insiders than outsiders, perhaps we could have adapted our intervention strategy and how we related to our client.

We work from the principle that change requires individuals to be in a learning frame and to feel that they have some mastery over their situation in the workplace. Through experience, we understand that if organizations are going to learn and grow, staff and management need to feel safe enough to be helped to learn and change. This is what we have put in place, for ourselves, as well as our clients. Our involvement with City Care has been an enormous learning opportunity for our whole organization. Our strong desire to provide a good service and assist the organization through the growth and all the challenges growth brings created a circumstance where, at times, we lost our own identity and purpose. We learnt much about ourselves, and were able to reflect that sometimes we needed to develop new processes and practices, and sometimes we just needed to get better at what we were doing. After our experiences with City Care, it would be reasonable to think that subsequent invitations would be met by a polite refusal. But our wariness of working with City Care was overcome by a greater need to help them assist *their* clients to gain better services.

Our ongoing involvement with City Care 'invitations' has changed not only our view of how we need to relate to other organizations, but also how we relate to ourselves.

The experience with City Care and a number of other organizations has led to us reflecting strongly on the role of the consultant in area of human services. To view ourselves as a relational consultancy means that the relationship allows *both client and consultant to craft changes in capacity, built through positive and negative reciprocal actions.* Each party affects the other in ways that should be meaningful and characterized by depth and longevity. We have found that, like other professionals working in contexts where they experience discord, distress and complexity, this work has a transformative effect on our staff that is akin to vicarious trauma. An important part of coping with the intensity of the work is to acknowledge the work will affect staff. So we seek to build protective measures to assist where challenging situations arise. These include:

- Increased knowledge of vicarious trauma.

- Strong ethical principle of practice.

- On-going training.

- Resolution of one's personal issues.

- Increased supervision and consultation.

- Competence in practice strategies.

- Good physical, emotional, social and spiritual self-care.

- Effective, open communication.

- Clear articulation and communication of the methods and processes of agency supports.

This chapter provided us with an invitation to share our journey of an organizational relationship that showed not only a client's vulnerability and learning but also our own.

Postscript

Jim called the other day – and invited us to work on an exciting new growth opportunity in New Zealand ... his last words were: 'What do you think?'

References

Ainsworth, M.D.S. and Bell, S.M. 1970. Attachment, exploration, and separation: Illustrated by the behavior of one-year-olds in a strange situation. *Child Development*, 41(1) (March, 1970), 49–67.

Anglin, J.P. 2002. *Pain, Normality and the Struggle for the Congruence: Re-Interpreting Residential Care for Children and Youth*. New York: Haworth Press.

Australia Unlimited Australian Government 2011 *Australia – A Story of Economic Strength and Resilience*. Available at: www.austrade.gov.au/../1358/Australias-economic-strengths.pdf.asp [accessed: 23 May 2012].

Bowlby, J. 1980. *Attachment and Loss (Vol. 3)*. New York: Basic Books.

Crittenden, P.M. 2006. A dynamic-maturational model of attachment. *Australian and New Zealand Journal of Family Therapy*, 27, 105–15.

Davies, R. 1997. Parallel processes in organizational consulting. *British Gestalt Journal*, 6(2), 114–17.

Gardiner, L. 2008. *Organizational Cultural Assessment & Profile OCAP*. SAL Consulting.

Gardiner, L., Summers, L. and Raftl, G. 2011. *Organizational Relational Assessment Tool ORAT*. SAL Consulting.

Hughes, D.A. 1997. *Facilitating Developmental Attachment: The Road to Emotional Recovery and Behavioral Change in Foster and Adopted Children*. Lanham, MD: Jason Aronson, Inc.

Klev, R. and Levin, M. 2012. *Participative Transformation: Learning and Development in Practising Change*. Farnham: Gower.

Raftl, G.C. 2005. *Facilitating Person-centred Self-determination: Formulating 'the Box' and Developing Integrated Understanding and Coordination in Support Design*. SAL Consulting.

Winnicott, D.W. 1965. *Maturational Processes and the Facilitating Environment: Studies in the Theory of Emotional Development*. London: Hogarth Press.

8

Too Close for Comfort: Attending to Boundaries in Associate Relationships

Karen Izod

Introduction

In any relationship with an organization as an external consultant or 'outsider', I can at times find myself behaving as an 'insider'. I might catch myself saying 'we' when I could have said 'you'. I might make use of a kind of insider savvy – the 'cutting to the chase' that comes with relating to a client and its system over time, where I find myself attached, both contractually and emotionally, with an organization, its people, and the work that it does.

This insider/outsider complexity in my relationships with clients is further compounded when I work in the role of an organizational associate. That is that I am engaged in delivering a range of interventions on behalf of an organization to which I am affiliated. This role, which frequently lacks contractual or task definition, occupies a position at the boundary of an organization, straddling the idea of 'insider' and 'outsider'. It seems to me to pose especial challenges in the way that it is taken up and negotiated, where the 'we' and the 'you' can be unclear and open to interpretation.

Quite what is meant by an 'associate' role with an organization is itself contested. In the writing of this paper I have been offered many descriptions and suggestions as to what its 'real' meaning is, based on local and specific examples. The *Oxford English Dictionary* (2007) suggests that an associate is someone who is 'joined in companionship, function and dignity', while also 'sharing in responsibility ... but with a secondary or subordinate status'. These descriptions offer some access to the array of dynamics that come into play in

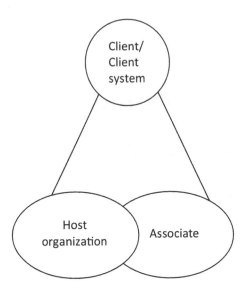

Figure 8.1   **Relational dimensions: Associate, client and host organizations**

attempting to take up associate roles, both at a feeling level – about who I am and how I am seen and valued – and at a contractual level – about what am I responsible for and the knowledge and practices I bring.

I am going to work with a definition for this chapter that an associate is part of a triangular relationship comprising self, as an independent practitioner, the 'host organization' to which the associate is 'joined' and to some extent represents, and a client system that is seeking services from the 'host'.

Here I am representing the associate and host organization as an overlapping entity, on equal terms, with rather more of me (as the associate) that is distinct and separate, yet enough of me that is joined to represent the host organization with credibility. The host organization and associate are additionally in a foreground/background relationship, which might also shift in relation to the client at different stages of the work. This representation depicts a set of relationships and characteristics operating conceptually and emotionally. As a model it offers a useful start in contracting for work as an associate, relating to the level of authority that I assume or negotiate in relation to the work with the client and how I might understand the nature of representation that is involved with the host organization.

A case involving Gwyneth is an example of a situation where I developed a close working relationship with a client and her system while working as an associate. The host organization had an existing relationship with the client and was able to bring me in as an associate with a particular knowledge base for a substantial and well-defined consulting assignment. I worked as the sole consultant with a high level of autonomy, occasionally consulting with the colleague in the host organization who had introduced me to the client to gain her perspective. Gwyneth said afterwards when we reviewed the work, 'Perhaps you did tell me that you were an associate, but it didn't especially register. I knew that you came recommended and that you were developing ideas in this field. The important aspect of the work was that we co-constructed the framework, you were influenced by me, and I was influenced by you – that shaped the way the project developed'.

I learned that the question of who I was and how I related to the host organization was not such an important issue for the client in this situation as it was for me. At one level, I knew my fit with this work was high, and I felt valued by client and host organization for the expertise that I could bring. At another level, I was concerned that I might not be experienced by the client as 'the real thing', but as secondary, a substitute. Within the host organization there was some debate as to why I had been asked to do the work, when it could have gone to an internal staff member. For my part, I found myself becoming meticulous about the rigour of my work: would it really stand up to scrutiny with the client and in the host organization? How could I bring what I knew to be good practice, but that would inevitably look different to what an internal staff member might do? The practice issue for me became one of the extent to which I needed to manage my image and reputation within the host organization, while also maintaining sufficient boundary to work well with the client.

In situations like this, it can be tempting for associates to close off the boundary with the host organization: in effect, to work in a quasi-independent role with the client, so as to limit the need to position the intervention within the host organization and to protect oneself from what can feel like additional emotional work. A harder, and usually invisible task, is to try to stay connected, and to search for some meaning in relation to this dynamic and what it might signify for the triad of relationships as a whole, and the consulting task that is being engaged with.

As I write about this experience, I'm aware of the desire for an ideal in choosing to begin with a mental model that suggests an equality in associate/ host relationship. This may well be serving as a mechanism for managing the tension outlined as 'joined … in dignity' while working 'in secondary or subordinate status'. The reality of associate relationships is rarely neat. A prolificacy of relationships and of hierarchical and status positions may operate over time between players, offering different degrees of insider/outsider connections for both host and client organizations.

Premise

My sense of the nature of associate relationships is that they are often formed on the basis of identifying with, or being in agreement with some aspect of the host organization, i.e., its principles, the way it does business, its theoretical stance. This is the side of associating that is about attraction through similarity, a meeting of minds, a 'keeping company'. But my proposition is that this similarity, which necessarily underpins the relationship, is insufficiently robust as a basis for a professional association. Inherent in similarity lies difference, something that acknowledges the capacity to be separate, differentiated, and other. Similarity and difference are complementarities (Benjamin 1997) and part of the same dynamic. Managing these tensions between similarity and difference, along with their associated power differentials, seems to be an essential feature in sustaining associate relationships for the benefit of the client system.

In this chapter, I shall be thinking about the associate role within the complex social and political changes that are occurring in the way people are employed and choosing to employ themselves. I will explore how taking up a role as an associate plays out at both contractual and relational levels and offer a number of vignettes from my practice as a consultant in organizational change and in the shadow consultancy and supervision that I offer to others who are practicing as associates. My intention is to draw from the voices of the associate, the host organization, and the client system, with the aim of teasing out and illustrating some of the dynamics involved and how we might bring a 'mind-ful' attentiveness (Whittle and Izod 2009) to our practice. In particular, I shall be looking at aspects of the associate role that require a capacity to differentiate one's skills and approaches from those of the host organization, as a means of managing some of the tensions inherent in the associate role which often involves actively experimenting with one's identity and role.

Why be an Associate?

The fictional detective Hercule Poirot (Christie 1920) almost always introduces Captain Hastings as 'my associate'. Just what is it that Captain Hastings does, and who is he in relation to Poirot? I would like to hear Hastings call Poirot 'my associate', to redress what, at least in the 1920s when these books were written, was some sense of proprietorial claim, the great detective and his rather incredulous, occasionally inspired companion. Of Hastings's own life and intentions we know very little. But their relationship exemplifies the act of associating with another that involves fellowship: they 'keep company' with each other for the common purpose of detecting crime. And in so doing, Hastings can access Poirot's world, take pleasure in and presumably benefit from his successes.

This kind of associating relationship might not stand up well nowadays, when we could expect Hastings to be more open about his own needs and ambitions, and when associations are more often between individuals and representatives of organizations. But yet elements of it persist in the reasons why professionals choose to work as associates. For self-employed, independent consultants, accompanying and journeying with an organization that espouses similar values, ideas and methodologies appeals. It can offer a sense of belonging with like-minded colleagues, mitigating some of the professional and personal isolation that working independently can bring. The host organization can attract with its market position, client list and actual or imagined potential. Power and reputation by association is often a seductive element, along with envisaged routes to market that may seem unavailable to the small, niche player. For individuals without established supporting infrastructures, associating with an organization so as to join forces can provide a combined, ideally more successful presence in the market, adding robustness in innovative project development and in competitive tendering and commissioning.

This is association from the perspective of the associate. For organizations, the taking on of associates can allow for leaner, more flexible organizational structures, a smaller core staff, keeping overheads and cash-flow demands to a minimum. As a pool of knowledgeable, seemingly compatible professionals, associates can provide accessible, reliable 'pairs of hands' (Block 2000) when facing particular short-term demands. Seeking out associates with particular skills can make up shortfall in the host organization, while associates with existing reputations and credentials in their field can provide cachet, an added 'pull' to prospective clients – just the reverse of the 'subordinate' position.

These individual and organizational choices take place in contexts of changing political and societal ideas about work, employment and being employed. Presently, the UK Coalition government is advocating a popular capitalism, suggesting that small business is a means of more directly equating contribution with reward, and pledging to 'remove the red tape' (www.conservatives.com) that prevents businesses from getting on and succeeding. This is a new stance on earlier neoliberal economic policies which changed the way that work and business could be done, i.e. bringing in internal economies within the public sector and imbuing their practices with entrepreneurial discourses.

For the individual, working patterns have also changed. Outsourcing of centralized or creative functions, which encourages small business start-ups or being employed back again as a 'freelance' worker in the same workplace in which one was made redundant, is commonplace (Storey et al. 2005). Fenwick (2001) describes the rise of 'workplace refugees': individuals, often women, choosing different values, different visions of success than those of their former employers. Sole trader, portfolio-holder, principal in my own business, are all identities taken up by individuals choosing to work alongside other organizations in a range of associative, partnership, sub-contracted and joint venture relationships – each with their own foreground/background dimensions in relation to the client.

What Does it Mean to be an Associate?

The question of 'what it means' to work as an associate frequently arises for me as I examine my own practices and those of colleagues and clients for whom I am a shadow consultant. I have talked so far about the dimensions of 'associating' that are emotional, relational and transactional, all of which can be located within a psychological contract (what we believe and imagine we are associating for) but rarely all located within a contract that is available for negotiation, whether that be written or spoken. These dimensions are explored in Walsh and Whittle's (2009) schema for understanding collaborative practice, which they outline in the interplay between: unconscious factors such as anxieties evoked in the work, defensive structures brought into play, and attachment patterns; subconscious factors such as trust, liking and power; and conscious factors such as tasks, roles and governance. They advocate for keeping open the collaborative space as a means of attending to the dynamics of collaboration in the moment.

In my experience of contracting for associate roles, this collaborative space is often contested, and managing the boundary between inner worlds of thoughts, feelings and fantasies, and outer worlds of roles and responsibilities is an ever-present dynamic. The 'space' for conceptualizing the nature of the association may be well defined and bounded where it is possible to outline expectations, acknowledge the mutual benefits of professional companionship and the mutual benefits to each other's businesses or livelihoods. Contracts may address issues such as intellectual property and 'ownership' of newly built client relationships in a way that acknowledges differentiated assets and investment of time and energies. Contracts may also be less defined and obscure, negotiated in processes of mutual adjustment (Mintzberg 1983), open to the interpretative structures of the key players and embodied in continuing negotiation about the distribution of resources, inputs and outcomes.

John was asked to do an internal piece of work for a consulting firm with which he worked as an associate organizational development consultant. One of the firm's consultants criticized John for not asking his advice in relation to difficulties which started to emerge in the consultation. John discussed the issue with me in my shadow consulting role. Looking at the detail of this, it became apparent that John was seeing this 'colleague' as part of his 'client system' and therefore located within his 'front-stage' (Goffman 1959) work. John was clear that he needed to carefully delineate his boundaries, managing his professional concerns about the work in 'back-stage' supervision and would have seen talking to this colleague as a breach of confidence. Meanwhile John's colleague felt excluded; he would much rather that John relate to him through participating in an informal network of relationships within the host organization where 'back-stage' work could be done in a collegial way. These are the kind of differences that individuals react to defensively and which then can be enacted at the level of the system. Splits between acceptable and unacceptable stances can then find their way into the triad of associate, host organization and client systems, including and excluding players in relation to the power dynamics between them.

Such issues can be addressed by thinking about quite what the role of associate is, and in particular, how (or whether) that is conveyed to the client system. Am I authorized to represent the host organization, and how much am I required to be consistent with their brand? Can I innovate and bring my own work in an 'equivalent reality' (Harris 2010: 22) rather than a representational way, yet which might still align with the espoused values of the organization? Is the client getting what they thought, or do they have a sense of having a substitute at best?

These tensions enter into how I as an associate construct my role and identity and how these in turn are constructed by others. They inevitably impact upon how I am able to work and my ability to effect change. How much of myself can and do I bring to the work? The idea of the 'enterprising self' (Du Gay 1996) is now well documented as a set of characteristics entailing the capacity to take risks, engage in continuous innovation, and take responsibility for one's professional development as an autonomous self. As much a call for employed staff working within entrepreneurial cultures, these characteristics are the everyday concerns of self-employed consultants. Organizations may well work with associates as a means of influencing or balancing what feels like overly dependent or passive modes of engagement with their employees, while at the same time, associates may seek to reduce the extent to which they have to do everything for themselves, looking for more supportive structures.

My experience is that these entrepreneurial behaviours are related to ambivalently by both the associate and the host organization, perhaps because they additionally speak to the question of belonging and the nature of 'joining' – 'do I really want to work here?' and 'do I really want to employ this person?' If the answer to these questions is yes, and if business rationales on both sides are supportive, then 'joining in dignity' is straightforward and the question of status can be negotiated through organizational structures and hierarchies. In situations where the answer to these questions is less than definitive, the nature of joining and of status is ambiguous.

Too Close for Comfort?

I'm returning now to the premise of forming a professional association in response to perceived similarities. Jennifer talked with me about just such an association. Very much a 'workplace refugee', Jennifer was in the process of establishing her own consulting practice. Well recognized in her original public sector domain, Jennifer was building reputation in community cohesion, making innovative links within and between organizations and sectors. Jennifer was invited to become an associate of a small consultancy firm moving into international development. The invitation related specifically to the design and delivery of a three-year project, through a public sector competitive tendering process. This offer had several appeals: the project fitted well with her specific skills and development needs, she liked and respected her colleague and his consulting company appeared to offer the 'back office' supports that the project needed and which Jennifer had yet to establish in her own practice. It felt like a sound platform for the work.

What did being an associate mean here? Jennifer found herself working much the same as she did in her own independent consultancy; she drew on her usual skills, created similar interventions, networked within the same networks, and in the process found herself working very much alone. Nothing new was being created through the association, and it felt increasingly difficult to collaborate to bring compatible but differentiated skills. Jennifer felt that she might just as well be working in her own consultancy, and further, that the work that she and her colleague did largely inhabited the same territory of roles, tasks and skills. With very little differentiation between what they were doing, and how they did it, they were 'too close for comfort'.

As the project continued, Jennifer found herself taking on more responsibility as her colleague's interest waned and as the resources from the company for this project competed for resources for other projects. 'Who am I building business for?' became the motif for her work. This host organization had wanted Jennifer to work as an 'insider', not differentiated from the company in the eyes of the client or the funding agency, so as to appear sufficiently coherent within the tendering process. In reality, while she acted as an 'insider' representing the host organization to the client and funders, she was operating at the boundary of their organization and her own. As these tensions intensified, it became more difficult to explore how to get the 'association' on a better footing and where the two key players could bring differentiated inputs. This is an association that may not last beyond the contracted term, and it could easily fall into the pool of associate work that ends with ill feeling.

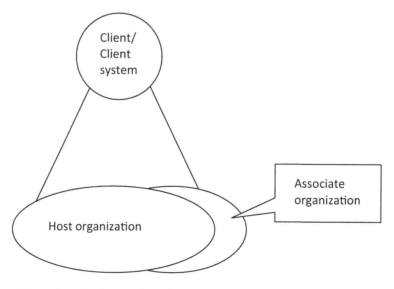

Figure 8.2   Jennifer's relational system

Jennifer's perception of her identity here is hardly different to her identity within her own consultancy. It is as if the two are interchangeable, and she could in many respects be working from her own company. Building some space between Jennifer and her colleague in terms of their roles and tasks is a starting point, aiming to create the kind of role flexibility and distinctiveness that would help them, and their client, to benefit from their association. This may be to take a risk, to access parts of their professional selves and organizational resources, which so far have not been able to make their way into the work, and which may come to have meaning for the project overall.

Part of the risk here, is, I think, about facing the ambiguities located in the association and the power differentials between the associates. There was the desire to set off on equal terms, each valuing the contribution of the other and their interdependence. Yet presenting themselves to the client as a single provider has become problematic. Jennifer has become increasingly visible to the client, almost as if she *is* the host organization, taking over many of the lead responsibilities for the work. At the same time, there is insufficient differentiated interaction between Jennifer and the host organization for their collaboration to be fully of service to the client. This prompts the wish that she could be doing this from her own company, coming out from behind the shadow of the host organization and working under her own business name. As things are, Jennifer encounters herself paradoxically as being barely visible, her own work going unrecognized.

For Jennifer and her colleague, finding a way to acknowledge the interdependence in their relationship might go some way to relieving the question of 'who am I building business for'. Both at some level knew that they would have been unlikely to win the work as single organizations, without the knowledge and experience in the one case, and the resources and infrastructure in the other, even if, now – some time into the contract – that is not so much the case. It can be helpful to work with interdependency in its split components – this is what I can work on independently, and this is what I am dependent upon, and, can I allow myself to occupy both these positions [Cleavely unpublished paper Saturn's Return to Heaven]. Allowing each other to occupy different positions in relation to these splits can bring a greater differentiation and hence variety to the work when it has blurred and lost its edge, as well as helping to surface the dynamics that are particularly difficult to address within the association.

But what if the contract with the client had been different? The host organization here is presenting itself to the client as the prime agency or contractor and Jennifer as part of that organization through association. When tendering processes privilege the single organizational provider, such an approach is a popular one. Yet, Jennifer could have been presented as a sub-contractor. Such a positioning might have enabled a more robust definition of roles and responsibilities and enabled Jennifer to work legitimately and visibly from her own consulting company. In business relationships that are formed through an affinity, or similarity of interests, declaring a hierarchy in relationships from the outset can be difficult, going against the grain of a joint entrepreneurial activity, with shared stakeholder interests. Yet, almost inevitably the power dynamic that emerges from one player needing to take a lead agency role in relation to a client will come to play out in a variety of ways over the life-cycle of the project, influencing the way in which consultants can manage their competition and contract within the system to bring their competence (Grueneisen and Izod 2009).

This example offers multiple possibilities for how work can be contracted for, within and between this triad of client, host organization and associate. Feelings have run high, and tensions encountered, not least to do with the nature of interdependence and the relative power of each of the players in deciding how things are done. At a dynamic level, is there anything that might have meaning for the system as a whole and the work that it is attempting to do? In the field of international development and aid, the question of who benefits, who does the work, who is visible and who is hidden is ever present: the nature of interdependence and relative power between these players is a factor in the way that work is done. In any developmental task there is always a likelihood that the work itself will come to take on characteristics and dynamics of the system it is engaged with. Until these dynamics can be surfaced, thought about and addressed, the potential for their enactment in both client and consultant systems is high (Izod 2003). Exploring these parallel processes between systems and the nuances of relationships between players can provide helpful data in furthering our understanding and insight into what might be at stake in attempting change.

Asking whether the situation that we encounter for ourselves bears any resonance within the client system is to form a hypothesis for exploration. I don't want to suggest that we might locate own contracting practices and dilemmas within the client but rather that the lens of the associate relationship can be helpful in thinking about what this might reflect of the client system and in turn how we contract and re-contract for the work and our continuing engagement in it.

Where is my Authority?

The ability to bringing a sufficiently differentiated approach to the host organization, while also acting under their brand, relies on being able to access an appropriate authority for the work, so as to be able to act in the moment for the benefit of the client. When I am faced with the tension between 'what am I expected to do here?' and 'what can I let myself do here?', I am aware that I am conceptualizing the host organization as taking up an intermediary space between myself and the client, filtering and shaping the nature of my contribution. I find that I need to challenge this construct to think about what the nature of representation is and whether, as I mentioned earlier, I can bring some kind of 'equivalent reality', recognizing that brand is a living and breathing entity, which I can influence as much as be influenced by.

David is a portfolio worker, managing a variety of consulting, coaching and media roles. With a preference for the immediacy of brief, here and now change interventions, he likes to work as an associate to a number of consulting companies that bring him in as a specialist within their existing contracts. They provide a route to market for David's expertise, without him needing to invest time in his own client-facing activities. David's contract is with the host organization, and he rarely is involved in negotiating contractual issues with the client system.

As part of a larger organizational change process, David was brought in to coach a diffident, and underachieving, Director in a pharmaceutical company.

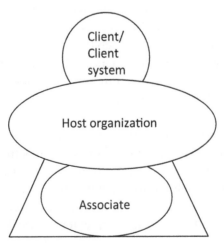

Figure 8.3   **David's relational system**

He soon realized that a few sessions would be insufficient to bring about the desired behavioural changes that all parties were hoping for. As he met with a disengaged client, showing little interest in his work or in the coaching process, David was concerned that nothing seemed to impress on his client, nothing seemed to take any purchase, and the work was stilted and uncomfortable. At the same time, David himself felt lack-lustre and would have liked to withdraw from the case.

David brought these concerns to supervision with me. We thought together about these dynamics as a 'counter-transference' (Klein 1946), the kind of batting to and fro of emotions between client/consultant that are indicative of both the mood of the work and what it is difficult to put words to. What *was* difficult for David to put words to was his own authority to act here. He had been engaged to work for a required number of sessions, towards a desired outcome. He now felt impelled to act differently, to deviate from his usual repertoire that he took on in this associate role and to work in a way that was more authentically himself. There was no contract for how David should behave. This is the part of the associate role which is often left unspoken and was an example of David's mode of 'associating' with the host company, where he felt that he had to represent something that was more planned and predictable but somehow leave out the part of himself that was more immediate and improvisational.

Taking David's experience further, as having potential meaning within the triad of players, we thought about the extent to which this coaching client himself felt authorized (or could authorize himself) to take more risks, to try things differently. And, how much the host organization itself felt able to raise the question of whether coaching was an appropriate intervention in this case. In the highly regulated world of pharmaceuticals, how much was it possible to experiment and seek out novel ways of doing things and to make changes in the moment that felt more generative of change?

David recognized that he was in a situation of drift, as was his individual client. In supervision we were able to talk about how he encountered the risks that he felt were located in working with greater authority in this contract. This involved checking out some assumptions with the host organization about his role, which in turn meant that some constraints about the work overall with the client system could be explored. David struggled with the idea that he was a 'jobbing consultant'. It wasn't an appealing term, but he also knew that working in this way presented a cost to his own sense of authority and freedom to act. How much this came with the role and how much he could negotiate so as to be able to work in his own equivalent reality was a tension. That David had to work on this for himself gave a sense of what it was that his client also had to manage in the way that he found himself taking up his own role.

Aspects of Trust and Control, Safety and Risk

I'd like to bring in now more of the voice from the client system, which in this case was also the host system. I was asked to design and deliver an 'in-house' intervention for a professional team within the organization where I held an associate role. As we reviewed this work some time afterwards, the following picture of safety and risk, trust and control emerged for both the commissioning client and for myself.

The Client's Voice – Karen is a tried and trusted colleague. I had seen her leading a workshop for the organization, which led me to believe that she could bring fresh perspectives to the developmental strategy I was constructing with my team. As an 'insider', she knew who some of the key characters were and some of the consequences of trying to make changes. She was familiar with the sectors that we worked with. The risks that I took in engaging her related to the pre-conceived ideas that team members might have of her and just how different her skills and approaches would be. At a time when the organization was divided in the way that it organized and rewarded its professional activities, she was seen as 'other', i.e., 'not us'. I didn't want this to become a factor for resisting the work, more an opportunity to look at things differently.

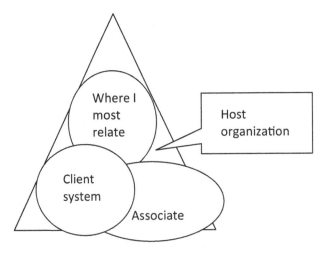

Figure 8.4   Working as a colleague

My Voice as Associate – My initial response was that this work posed me with a dilemma as to whether I should accept it. At some level it felt too close for comfort: my work would be very visible and my reputation at stake. In terms of a fit with my consulting abilities, the task of enabling a team to work on its development strategy was familiar, but some of the language in use and concepts that it valued felt alien. It represented a challenge in straddling organizational cultures, much as would be the case with an external client, and I realized that I had bought into the construction of 'them as other'. I was undoubtedly anxious about taking on the work and realized that I had to work on my own containment: could I suspend my own experiences of how things were done in the organization enough to access this team's experiences, and could I separate myself enough from performance/outcome issues to have sufficient access to my consulting repertoire? In other words, could I take up this role with credibility?

At the time, the client's concerns about how I might be received by her team were not fully articulated. As an associate on the boundary, I hadn't realized how much I was being identified with the unit that I was involved in, or indeed, how much I had identified with them. I had imagined that I was seen as functioning more independently. Yet I could feel the reputational risk involved, the need to be open and receptive to the client's preferred ways of doing things, while also working from a position that felt authentic. I was aware that I needed to access a mode of relating (language, concepts) that was sufficiently similar so as not to alienate, yet also sufficiently different to be able to stimulate (new language, new concepts). We were then both having to attempt something similar, to jointly take a risk.

What, if anything, helped to contain these reputational risks and concerns? Kitay and Wright (2003) talk of the Partner role, a trusted external provider, who needs to draw on the networks of relationships and the social system of the client organization in order to achieve their work. To some degree, knowing members of the client system through informal exchanges meant that a high level of collaboration in the planning stages was possible. This in turn meant that some of the projections involved in us/them could be managed at the point of delivery of the workshop, where the boundary between 'me as associate' and 'them as client' was more marked. Collectively our task was to manage issues of trust, and so relinquish some control, and to take some risks which involved giving up safer ways of doing things. In that sense, I had to be willing to bring a riskier version of myself, not just the person that I was perceived as being – which contributed to the trust, but a person that could have a different repertoire to them. I needed to access and make available an identity in consulting other than through the host organization, one that involved an entrepreneurial self, that could manage our difference as much as our similarity.

Where Now?

Consulting from an associate role is about consulting with one's feet (and mind) straddling several boundaries: those involving the client and their systems and those involving the host organization. These examples of associate work and the challenges that they pose illustrate how such boundaries can often be unclear, or become unclear, as the work shifts and relationships adapt and change. Attending to these shifts and changes so as to maintain the capacity to work in role in relation to the client system is a key aspect of working in associative relationships. In that sense, working as an associate is as much about a mode of relating, of 'associating', as about doing. The 'association' can serve as a touchstone in the mind to which one has thoughts, feelings and fantasies, which may come to have meaning for the nature of the work that one can do, and through which it is possible to project one's imagination and creativity, one's needs and anxieties.

As I write this, I see that this is the language of attachment (Bowlby 1969), the need for a secure base so as to manage anxiety in relation to one's identity and capacity to do the work. But this is a complex attachment, particularly because of the ambivalence evoked through interdependency. I've suggested earlier that this relates to an ambivalence about employment, 'do I want to work here?' and 'do I want to employ this person?' This is at the rational level but underneath this lies the primary risk (Hirschhorn 1999) of pursuing the enterprise: that if I work as an associate, then I may be consumed by the host organization and so lose my identity and reputation and that if the host organization invites this associate in to work with them, then they run the risk of losing identity through merger [Whittle personal communication]. This represents the primary risk of associate relationships, where the mode of engagement is primarily through accessing the 'entrepreneurial self' (Du Gay 1996) and the fantasies and realities of roles which value the autonomous but require mutual and inter-dependent relations.

My central premise for this chapter has been that many associate relationships are formed on the basis of a mutual attraction or similarity but that the capacity to differentiate to be 'other' is essential. This means that there will often be a sense of being on an edge, of belonging and not belonging to the host organization, of managing feelings of not quite being legitimate in the work, while also finding ways to access appropriate authority. I would like to propose that working at this edge, managing the need to be joined but separate and individuated, offers a creative tension in the work and may often be a reason why associate relationships persist when a less complex sub-contractor role might be easier to manage.

But this is to individualize the situation. Lawrence and Robinson's (Lawrence and Robinson 1973) concept of the primary task may be helpful in exploring the link between the individual and the host organization in relation to the work they attempt together. They offer a heuristic device to identify the stated primary intention of an organization (the normative), what people say and believe they are doing in pursuit of a livelihood (the existential) and the unconscious tasks that are being pursued by organizational members as a defensive system against anxiety (the phenomenological). This device can be utilized in thinking about how and what to contract for: is the normative rationale for the association valid, what other forms of relating might be appropriate in the business context; what is happening at the existential level? Are tasks and beliefs in any way congruent with intention? The phenomenological is inevitably more difficult to bring to the surface, becoming apparent in processes of interaction, as patterns of behaviours start to coalesce into acceptable and unacceptable behaviours in role. As with the example of John, the extent to which associates make use of the supportive structures of the host organization, as a kind of external internal, is a feature here. This will have a bearing on the potential for utilizing the unconscious defensive structures of the organizational system (Menzies Lyth 1960) in support of the associate relationship or the extent to which the associate has to remain firmly 'other': relying on their own emotional resources, capable of receiving unwanted, unconscious feelings projected into them from the host organization, and similarly of displacing and projecting their own.

Such an analysis of primary task(s) in relation to the association can go some way to illuminating the relatedness between the client system and the host organization, within the triad of associate relationships. It can offer a helpful perspective in relation to what the parties might need to confront to effect change. This isn't to suggest that there are immediate parallels between individual or dyadic players, rather more that there might be angled mirrors, catching the reflections of others, allowing for a further level of sensemaking in the task of consulting to change.

Acknowledgements

I would like to acknowledge the contributions of Evelyn Cleavely, Christine Davies, Veronika Grueneisen, Dione Hills, Phil Lowe and Juliet Scott in the writing of this chapter.

References

Bartholomew, K. and Horowitz, L.M. 1991. Attachment styles among young adults: a test of a four-category model. *Journal of Personality and Social Psychology*, 61(2), 226–44.

Benjamin, J. 1997. *Shadow of the Other. Intersubjectivity and Gender in Psychoanalysis.* New York: Routledge.

Block, P. 2000. *Flawless Consulting: A Guide to Getting your Expertise Used.* 2nd Edition. New York: Jossey-Bass/Pfeiffer.

Bowlby, J. 1969. *Attachment and Loss: Volume 1.* London: Hogarth Press and the Institute of Psychoanalysis.

Christie, A. 1920. *The Mysterious Affair at Styles.* Introduces Hercule Poirot and Captain Hastings. Lodnon: John Lane.

Conservatives.com. Describes present UK government strategy to supporting small businesses. Available at: http://www.conservatives.com/News/News _stories/2011/03/Government_bins_red_tape_for_small_businesses.aspx [accessed 27 May 2012].

Du Gay, P. 1996. *Consumption and Identity at Work.* London: Sage.

Fenwick, T. 2001. Knowledge and the enterprising self: Workplace refugees navigating entrepreneurial discourses. *Studies in the Education of Adults*, 33(2), 127–34.

Goffman, E. 1959. *Presentation of Self in Everyday Life.* New York: Anchor Books.

Grueneisen, V. and Izod, K. 2009. Power dynamics of expertise and containment in the process of hiring and being hired. *Mind-ful Consulting*, edited by S. Whittle and K. Izod. London: Karnac Books, 57–74.

Harris, A. 2010. *Romantic Moderns: English Writers, Artists and the Imagination from Virginia Woolf to John Piper.* London: Thames Hudson Ltd.

Hirschhorn, L. 1999. The primary risk. *Human Relations*, 52(1), 5–23.

Izod, K. 2003. *Book Review: 'Enactment, Toward a New Approach to the Therapeutic Relationship'*, edited by S.J. Ellman and M. Moskowitz (Lanham, MD: Aronson, 1998). *Journal for Organisational and Social Dynamics*, 3(1), 170–74.

Kitay, J. and Wright, C. 2003. Expertise and organizational boundaries: The varying roles of Australian management consultants. *Asia Pacific Business Review*, 9(3), 21–40.

Klein, M. 1946. Notes on some schizoid mechanisms. *International Journal of Psycho-Analysis*, 27, 99–110.

Lawrence, W.G. and Robinson, P. 1973. An innovation and its implementation: Issues of evaluation. Tavistock Institute of Human Relations Document no. CASR 1069, unpublished.

Menzies Lyth, I. 1960. A case-study in the functioning of social systems as a defense against anxiety: A report on a study of the nursing service of a general hospital. *Human Relations*, 13(2), 95–121.

Mintzberg, H. 1983. *Structures in Fives: Designing Effective Organizations*. Upper Saddle River, NJ: Prentice Hall.

Oxford English Dictionary, (shorter) Sixth Edition 2007. Oxford: Oxford University Press.

Storey, J., Salaman, G. and Platman, K. 2005. Living with enterprise in an enterprise economy: Freelance and contract workers in the media. *Human Relations*, 58(8), 1033–54.

9

Theory for Skilled Practitioners

Robin C. Stevens

This book of tales from the field is purposefully short of extensive discussion of the theory that underpins the thinking embedded in the chapters. All of the practitioners who have shared their work in this book, however, draw on theories that are informed by psychoanalysis, group relations work, and the science of open systems. Accordingly, the editors thought that it would be useful to include a chapter that foregrounds some of the theories relevant to understanding organizational change from within. Well-known theories applying psychoanalytic concepts to illuminate interactions in the workplace and to understand group processes, the behaviour of people in groups, and the application of open systems theory to organizations were developed through the work of the Tavistock Institute in London. In the United States, these concepts found a home in the Organization Program of the William Alanson White Institute of Psychiatry, Psychoanalysis & Psychology in New York City.

The authors of this book have chronicled frankly many difficulties they have faced in their efforts to consult effectively to organizational change. They have described the pushes and pulls they experience in their relationships with individual organization members, with members of particular groups and as group members themselves. They have narrated their struggles to maintain their effectiveness as consultants when they are employees or management team members of the organization they consult to or when, as externals, they have consulted to an organization so intimately that they feel a part of it. I think that theories drawn from psychoanalysis, group relations work, and open systems theory illuminate very well the challenges that consultants, particularly insider consultants whose boundary position is contested in so many ways, face in helping organizations change. These theories deal with the feelings of belonging, of outsider-ness, of what it means to be inside an organization, to be affected by other people – in short, with what it means to be human and to be a part of the complexity that is an organization.

Psychoanalytic theories assert that emotions do not reside exclusively in an individual but may be distributed throughout a human system. They can be evoked in others (Hirschhorn 1988): if I feel something when I'm consulting to a client, it's likely that the people I'm working with feel corresponding emotions. If I feel parental, then it is likely that the people sitting in front of me seeking help are feeling dependent. If I am feeling confused, it's likely that others feel the same way, too. If I feel a sense of dread, it's likely that the feeling is shared. Emotions provide data about what is happening in the workplace (Hirschhorn 1988) and are therefore worth being mind-ful of (Whittle and Izod 2009) in order to manage or consult more effectively. The authors of this book have learned to be mind-ful about their own feelings and to identify them to obtain information about what their clients are feeling.

Psychoanalytic theories cover dynamics at various levels of organizational life: intra-personal, inter-personal, group, inter-group and inter-organizational (Wells 1985). They and theories about group behaviour and systems thinking are useful to insider consultants in making sense of organizational dynamics that otherwise remain below the radar and that can impede or derail change efforts. They offer consultants concepts that help them and their clients become more aware of the dynamics that affect their work together and help consultants to be more intentional in their actions. This chapter refers to earlier chapters in this book to show how contributors have used these theories in their work.

First, I discuss theories that draw on psychoanalytic thinking: how emotions affect individuals and work groups involved in change processes. Then I turn to the role of anxiety and how containment enables productive work. Next, I discuss the contributions that derive from group relations work: the concepts of boundary, authority, role and task (BART) that help illuminate authority relationships, define working relationships, and spot and understand disconnects about who is doing what, for what purpose and with whom. I look at the influence of open systems theory on the understanding of the workplace and organizational change and in particular the notion of sentient systems. Finally, I discuss how the consulting practices depicted in this book are informed by some of these concepts.

Managing Anxiety and Offering Containment

Anxiety plays a central role in how organization members manage their work (Hirschhorn 1988). Some anxiety is helpful. Too much and people cannot work effectively. Where does anxiety come from? Well, sometimes from the work itself. In Chapter 3, Pauline Holland notes the 'primitive anxieties' that working with 'children and young people involved in offending behaviour' stirs up in staff members. Anxiety may come from projects that have high risk or make or break significance (Stevens and Whittle Chapter 4). It may come when some family members do not want, but need, to confront one another (Wigutow Chapter 6) or when a CEO is accused by his staff of 'dining with the devil' (Adebowale Chapter 2). A consultant may find herself flooded with anxiety about her ability to help a client (Stevens and Whittle Chapter 4). Finding ways to contain anxieties is a significant challenge when changing organizations from within. Change often involves a loss of familiar ways of doing things, a loss of a sense of mastery (Marris 1974). Even when change is desired, it often involves loss.

Skilled practitioners find ways to help organization members contain felt anxieties and tensions by creating some psychological safety or what Winnicott refers to as a holding environment (Winnicott 1986). In Chapter 1, Andrew Day discusses making a point of using familiar business language when discussing options with organization members to help them in the process of acknowledging the tensions they were experiencing. He chose that in preference to having a discussion about the psychodynamics he observed in order to 'minimize the risks of playing into splits'. Framing the issues in business language enabled the people involved to acknowledge the legitimacy of their differing positions. He also notes that they decided to meet with each business unit separately to report their findings in an effort to contain their anxiety about the change process. Meeting in larger, mixed groups might have led to immediate jockeying for position, with participants afraid to ask questions and discuss their concerns and ideas for fear of showing weakness. The program could easily have gone awry for reasons having nothing to do with the merits. In Chapter 4 on project management, Sue Whittle and I write about what happened when work group representatives worked together to create project workflows: the process provided space for junior staff members to ask questions of their managers in a more collaborative context than that where a manager reviews a subordinate's work. The environment provided containment for anxieties that all participants may have felt about revealing that they had questions about how to do their jobs. We use the film *The King's Speech* and describe how the speech therapist contained the Prince's anxieties by reframing his impossible task (Chapter 4 in this book).

Uncovering the tensions present in an organization and understanding how organization members think of them is challenging. The presenting problem, or how what needs attention is described, is only part of the story. Each organization member will have a different view of the organization and its problems. That view will encompass both the social facts (Durkheim 1982) of the organization and a person's projections and feelings about the organization. A shorthand way of referring to this is the 'organization-in-the-mind' (Armstrong 2005). A classic projective exercise to help reveal the different ways that organization members relate to their organization is to ask each to draw a picture (using newsprint and coloured markers) of their role in the organization (or of a work dilemma they are experiencing). Then post the drawings on the walls, have people do a 'gallery walk' to look at the different ways that people depict the same organization, and then discuss what people have noticed. This exercise starts to put people in touch both with their own experience (people can be surprised by what they see in their own drawings) and those of others. The drawings often reveal the projections people have about other organization members or units. Do they put themselves at the centre or way out on the edge? Are they in a boat or drowning? Do they draw themselves with multiple arms pulled tight in every direction? Is another unit portrayed as a black cloud? Talking about the drawings can begin a process of checking out the reality and the range of the organizations-in-the-mind in a group and offer a checklist for which anxieties need containment. A key component of work to manage and contain anxiety is helping clients see the dynamics. Ronald Heifetz (1994) talks about getting on the balcony to see the swirl of events so as to be able to see how they affect work. Sally R. Wigutow discusses the challenge of helping clients develop the capacity to see the tensions and systems at play as a first step to being able to talk about them. Facilitating the discussion of the situations that cause us pain, embarrass us, or make us feel vulnerable (Argryis 1994) is an important skill for practitioners.

Recognizing Emotions at Work

Our tales from the field have demonstrated that organizational change is much more than the rational management of task and that understanding the emotions at play is a valuable skill for practitioners. Freud first described psychoanalytic processes in relation to individuals. They are now widely seen as present in/relevant to groups as well. Some of the processes that are especially significant in organizational life are transference, splitting, projection and introjection.

TRANSFERENCE

Our earliest experiences as infants and children are particularly important to the way we are in the world, including the way we are in organizations: how we relate to colleagues, what roles we prefer, what tasks we are drawn to and which we avoid. Our families of origin are our first organization and their imprint is profound (Singer and Shapiro 1989). How we encounter workplace dilemmas is influenced by family experiences. I may experience something as a dilemma as you would. Or, confronted with the same issue, we may have different takes on it because each of us has learned different ways of coping. We will have different modes for taking up authority or speaking up and we will have grown used to taking up different roles (e.g., peacemaker, the silent one, leader) in our families of origin. Earl, a colleague of mine, was troubled when a woman who worked for him told him she had real difficulty telling him that she wanted to leave for a better job – one that paid more and gave her a challenging opportunity in a different field. She told Earl that she thought he would be mad at her for wanting to leave. Earl asked me how she could think that when he is so mild-mannered. I said maybe she wasn't relating to him as Earl but as someone from her past. Perhaps the situation had evoked the feelings she had when asking her father or mother for something she really wanted. She wasn't seeing him for who he was in that moment. When I observe a client acting in a way that seems strange to me, I might ask the client whether the situation feels like something she has experienced before to establish whether we are dealing with some transference from her past. It helps the client notice what has been out of her awareness: the fact that these unconscious feelings from past experience '… dictate irrational responses to the present' (Frosch 2003: 89). This gives us the data to talk about how the past may be getting in the way of the present.

In Chapter 6, Sally offers an example of how earlier relationships are re-enacted in present situations. We hear how David, the owner of a ball-bearing manufacturing plant, may have enacted his childhood relationship with his younger sister when he was angry about her reasonable request to go with him on his next sales trip so that she could meet the company's biggest customers. Sally notes that she became aware of how David and his sister may have confused work and sibling roles saying:

> *I became aware of this confusion through my own internal experience of their interaction wanting to speak out to my sense of self-righteousness on her behalf. I felt the push and pull of familiar roles from my family experience, of gender issues, and of memories of my own family's business[.] (Chapter 6).*

She demonstrates the value that practitioners can bring when they are aware of and curious about the transferences between their clients and them. Sally states that just as her prior experiences influence what she sees and feels in the client system, she is aware that how her clients experience her is dependent on their prior experiences and that it may take time for them to experience her as she is. When another David, the portfolio worker in Karen Izod's chapter (8) about associate relationships, finds it difficult to authorize himself to act to negotiate a better work arrangement, he may have been re-enacting previous relationships where he also had trouble looking after his own interests.

SPLITTING

Splitting is a defence that helps us cope in situations with high degrees of complexity or ambiguity. To protect ourselves from being overwhelmed or having to deal with that complexity or ambiguity, we split an object into all good or all bad. Seeing things in black or white avoids the work of having to deal with shades of grey. In Andrew Day's case about a business alliance (Chapter 1), he notes that he and his colleague entered their client system toward the bottom of the power structure. He says that if they had negotiated a contract with the CEO, they would have had an opportunity to 'understand his agenda' and 'secure his support for engaging his peers'. This view about how things might have gone seems to split off any possibility that the CEO might well have not been forthcoming and in fact may have obscured some of his motives. This split may have stemmed from an idealization of the CEO and his power and a concomitant devaluation of the consulting skills that Andrew and his colleague brought to the task. In Victor O. Adebowale's chapter (3), the senior managers initially reacted to the idea of business concerns operating in the social service sector as all bad. These all or nothing views are evidence of splits.

Splits are often in evidence when projects get into trouble: people learn to mask painful feelings about their own ability to manage or anxiety about situations where they feel increasingly out of control with strongly held views that another party is the cause of the problem when in truth problems are rarely so black and white. If I am aware that personal feelings like these might be at the root of my client's intense dislike of another project participant, I am more able to be useful to them in helping them think critically about the situation in order to address it effectively.

PROJECTION

People use projective processes to help manage their anxiety (Hirschhorn 1988). The process happens at an unconscious level. Projection allows people to foist anxiety on others rather than own it themselves. While we were working on this book, my co-editor sent an email to all the authors suggesting that we share drafts of chapters to identify links between themes. I immediately replied privately to her that I was sure that one of the authors I was editing would not want to do so since she felt that she was nearly finished with her chapter and wouldn't want to have to consider other authors' comments. The next morning my author emailed all the authors attaching a copy of her chapter and inviting others' comments. Clearly, I had projected my own anxieties onto her. I did not want to own my anxiety about putting my work out for comment and projected my feelings onto another author. If only she had joined my efforts to put the kibosh on sharing work, I might not have had to face my anxiety!

A manager may project her own feelings of competence onto her boss in an effort to avoid having to engage in decision-making that makes her anxious. If she can get him to make decisions, she can avoid the anxiety. The boss may suddenly feel the need to make decisions he previously had thought his subordinate was in the best position to make. Helping them both to recognize what is happening so that they can identify and talk about the anxiety that impels her to give away her competency is everyday work for consultants who practice psychoanalytically. It takes skill to recognize what is going on and to know that one is being invested with an attribute not one's own. The consultant acts in a non-anxious way to provide a holding environment to contain the employee so she can do the work of changing (Winnicott 1986). In Chapter 7, Lisa Gardiner and colleagues discuss the support that SAL Consulting provides to its consultants to help them understand and work through the difficult dynamics they encounter when consulting to organizations providing social services to people with complex problems. The consultants working with the organization gather in facilitated meetings to reflect as a group on the way work is going and what they are experiencing and to plan for the future. The process creates a holding environment (Winnicott 1986) that facilitates more effective work with client organizations that are stressed by the 'primitive anxieties' (as Pauline Holland puts it (Chapter 2)) arising from such work.

INTROJECTION

Someone on the receiving end of a projection may introject it and act as if the emotion projected were their own: My employees are anxious about the potential outcome of a meeting I am going to participate in. I pick up on their anxiety. I introject it and although I was not worried about the meeting before, I am now. This happens unconsciously and often at lightning speed. Alternatively, an individual may recognize a projection and deflect it. If I am able to recognize that the anxiety I am feeling is my client's and not my own and so not introject it, I will be better able to help the client understand and work through his anxiety.

Working with Emotions in Groups

Often, consulting and organizational development work focuses on the development of intra-personal qualities and skills and on inter-personal relationships. However, groups are ubiquitous in organizational life and understanding their dynamics offers consultants another perspective in working with their clients. I turn now to the contribution of group relations theories to understanding how the dynamics of groups shape organizational change. The theories I discuss concern the nature of groups and how people behave in them; I also offer examples of how consultants might intervene where group dynamics interfere with task accomplishment.

In the 1940s, Wilfred Bion, a British psychoanalyst, made a major contribution to our understanding of organizational change with his theories about behaviours in groups. He noticed that groups are more than collections of individuals, that they have a life of their own, and that unconscious processes influence how they operate (Bion 1961). In Chapter 5, Sue Whittle writes about a group that consistently, and without conscious intent, talked until time was up without completing its task. The internal consultant often found herself stepping into an expert role and solving the problem in the remaining time. One time she described this recurring pattern of behaviour and suggested that the group reconvene the next day, since productive work seemed to have ceased. Shocked, the group completed the task in the time remaining. Bion's theories about basic assumption (Ba) behaviour help us to understand that the group was dealing with anxiety about its task by avoiding the task and sucking the consultant into problem-solving mode to do it for them. The consultant's intervention allowed group members to see what they were doing and get back on task.

Individuals may seek to avoid the anxiety of functioning as a work group, that is, a group operating at a rational level to address their task, by engaging in Ba behaviour (Bion 1961). The change from work group to Ba group and back again happens almost instantaneously and at an unconscious level. Bion described three kinds of Ba behaviours: Ba dependence, where all individuals in the group behave as if they have an exclusive relationship with the leader who will protect them from their fears; Ba fight/flight, where group members engage in fights not related to the work or take flight from their task; and pairing, where members of the group act as if the pairing of two group members will produce some idealized future. When a work group faced with a difficult issue on a tight deadline spends much of that time in gales of laughter about the way that others behave or chooses to work on their resentment towards another department, contractor, or competitor rather than getting on with the job, it is probably a sign that the group is engaged in Ba fight/flight behaviour. The group that never completed its task described above was engaging in Ba dependency behaviour. An 'essential part' of this regressive dynamic is '[t]he belief that a group exists, as distinct from an aggregate of individuals ... and that the individuals involved believe and behave as if they are a group' (Bion 1961: 142). To help group members back to functioning as a work group, someone might say, 'It seems to me that we're having a difficult time staying on track. I wonder what is going on'. This may be enough to give group members the space to notice they are off task. An insider consultant familiar with basic assumption dynamics could be more direct and say, 'We've been off topic for the last 15 minutes or so. It seems to me that the work we've been asked to do is so daunting that it's easier for us to avoid it by telling stories'. In each instance, the consultant intervenes into the way the group is working with emotions arising from anxiety. A key is to give the group space to reflect on and discuss what is happening so that the anxiety is publicly acknowledged.

Like individuals, groups can split off uncomfortable feelings and project them onto others. Sometimes this facilitates the work of the group; other times, it impedes it (Bion 1961). When a company faces an unexpected competitive challenge, its executive team may ascribe superior powers to know how to handle the situation to the CEO: this may be helpful in enabling individuals to act as a team. It also may be unhelpful, by silencing individuals at precisely the time the company could benefit from their multiple perspectives on the challenges they face. The CEO may introject the attribution of superior skills because it helps him deal with his own feelings of anxiety. When Victor O. Adebowale entered Community Therapy as its new CEO (Chapter 3), board members may have split off their feelings of anxiety about the organization's future and their roles in it. Victor may have deflected those projections (we don't hear that he felt unduly anxious) and not assumed all the work of worry on himself, choosing instead to lead board members in strategic debates about the organization's future.

In Andrew Day's case about corporate governance (Chapter 1), he observes that people in the business units projected their feelings of incompetence onto the alliance managers. By doing this, the business unit staff could rid themselves of their felt inadequacy about having to deal with the complexity of managing relationships with others involved in the alliance.

The Tavistock Institute developed group relations conferences as a means to study groups and their behaviours (Hayden and Molenkamp 2002). The Tavistock and other organizations around the world sponsor such conferences today. Attendees have the opportunity to study the effects of projective processes on themselves and others. A process that participants often learn to understand in conferences is that one person can 'carry something' for the group: in other words, the group can find expression in the actions of one person whom the group, acting unconsciously, has tasked to represent it (Wells 1995). Here's a story from Wells about this phenomenon: one of the students in a class was continuously disruptive. The teacher thought he should go into a special class for disturbed children. With the student's departure, another pupil began to disrupt the class. Eventually, he, too, was sent to the special class. The teacher had analyzed the behaviour at an intrapersonal level. No sooner had the second child left than a third child began to disrupt the class. Group-level analysis reveals that the group – the class – was using one child after another to express its dissatisfaction with the class and the teacher. By using one child to express the group's feeling, the other children could appear to be well behaved.

Pauline Holland writes in Chapter 2 of the concern that internal consultants were '… soaking up a lot of the organization's mess' in her organization. From a group relations perspective, we might notice how the anxieties of working with difficult populations have been dumped on the organization's internal consultants. In selecting whom to mobilize to work on the group's behalf, a group may pick up on a person's valency to assume a particular role (Wells 1995). In Pauline's organization (Chapter 2), organization members may have unconsciously believed that the internal consultants were the most able to handle the organization's anxiety. In the case in Chapter 7, SAL consultants, even though they are externals, work so closely with their client organization that they pick up the anxieties that organization members experience in their work with vulnerable people. To help its consultants work effectively, a core part of SAL's work is providing containment (Bion 1961) for their anxieties through meetings and work activities to discuss and reflect on the client's dynamics. This can help the consultants understand what part of the anxieties they feel is the result of the client's projective processes.

One way that practitioners make use of their observations about behaviour in groups is through process consultation (Schein 1988). Process consultants comment on a group's processes – how members of a group do things and avoid doing things. This helps members become aware of their group processes and how they affect work. The aim is for members of the groups to use that understanding to work in more effective ways. A process comment might be:

> *I notice that in this meeting and in the two before it, only the CEO and the same two of the twelve people present have spoken, but as soon as the meeting is over, I hear many more people talking about the topic in the hallways as they return to their offices. What might be preventing more people from speaking up during the meeting?*

This mode contrasts with consultants who take up their roles as experts or as a pair of hands (Schein 1988). Consultants who have an understanding of group processes have the skill to draw clients' attention to a broader range of behaviours than consultants who understand groups primarily at an intra- or interpersonal level. Pauline Holland (Chapter 2) describes how internal consultants worked with teams to help them understand how their anxieties about changes in the external environment and about their work with disturbed people affected their work.

The Power of Group Membership and Identity

A key concept related to groups is the idea of sentient groups. These are groups (real and imagined) to which we feel committed and turn to for emotional support (Miller and Rice 1990). We say that we have sentient ties when we feel connected to people as a result of group membership. We may have sentient ties coincident with identity or organizational groups but not necessarily. Different experiences of groups might include: I am born into my family but I do not turn to them for emotional support. I am of Irish heritage and relate easily to someone else of Irish heritage, whatever their age or line of work. I work in the engineering department at my company and feel loyalty to the department and its members. I started in the law department of my organization but now work in human resources and have for several years. I am still in touch with former colleagues in the law department and seek their help more frequently than do my colleagues in HR. In this instance, sentient ties probably arise out of membership in a profession as well as having worked in the same department.

Group memberships affect work. They divide into two categories: identity groups and organizational groups (Alderfer 1987). Identity groups include those we are born into such as family, gender, religion and race; those who are affected by similar historical experiences, such as people who experienced the Great Depression or the 1960s; and those who have undergone the same social experience, such as having worked for a company that went out of business. People in such groups would be likely to share some world views. Organizational groups are ones where members work at similar levels in the organization or have the same work experience and therefore also are likely to share world views. These could include an executive team that steered a firm through a crisis or engineers who worked together on a major project for a number of years. Alderfer notes that there is likely to be a correlation, depending on culture, of identity and organizational groups. For example, in some organizations, white men hold most of the key executive positions while members of minority groups and women tend to hold lower ranking, less central positions. Noticing the groups, who is included and who excluded, and on what basis, can offer valuable insights into what needs to change and what can change. Sally R. Wigutow (Chapter 6) uses a three-circle diagram as a diagnostic tool to help organization members in family businesses see and understand how membership of family, owner and manager groups affects what they and others do and how. Is the son who chafes at his mother's leadership of the firm acting as a son or as a junior staff member? Sally concludes that the son's ambivalence at working with his mother as boss stemmed from family tensions that were compounded by unclear business roles.

Group-level projections often come into play around membership and identity (Alderfer 1987). The non-family members of a business may have different projections about the executive team composed solely of family members and their handling of an employee issue than they would if the executive team had an equal representation of family and non-family members. Alderfer writes:

> By viewing transactions between individuals from an intergroup perspective, an observer learns to examine the condition of each participant's group, the relationship of participants to their groups, and the relationship between groups represented by participants as well

as their personalities in each 'interpersonal' relationship[.] (Alderfer 1987: 203).

External consultants who feel like insiders may find themselves excluded from certain discussions; before ascribing the exclusion to someone's thoughtlessness, they may want to consider the effect that non-membership in the organization has had on the decision to exclude. Karen Izod considers her group memberships and how they affect her work as an associate (Chapter 8). In the vignette involving her client Gwyneth, Karen worries about her status as associate, concerned that Gwyneth will think of her as 'less than' an employee of the host organization. This concern leads Karen to be meticulous about the work, only to find out that Gwyneth is hardly aware of her group membership. Might Karen have been even more effective if she'd been free of her insider/outsider anxieties? More freewheeling?

Recognizing how sentient ties affect both my client and me is a useful skill for consultants. Sally discusses in Chapter 6 how her own group memberships – outsider to the family, sometimes perceived as an insider to the business, and her identity characteristics – pull her into or push her away from relationships with one person or with one group or another.

BART: A Way to Understand Organizations

One way of understanding organizations that is particularly helpful in consulting to change from within, involves the concepts of boundary, authority, role and task or 'BART' (Green and Molenkamp 2005). They view boundary as '… the container for group work[.]' and advocate for the study of boundaries associated with '[t]ime, task, and territory' (2). They note the many dimensions that boundaries have. They can be physical: people may have different working relationships with other organization members depending on whether they work on the same floor or not; those who wear headphones may work very much as isolates compared to those who overhear hallway conversations. Boundaries can be psychological: even though the senior managers in Community Therapy worked in the same organization as the executive group, they did not feel allied with them (Chapter 3). The term 'sentience' refers to feelings of belonging and loyalty to a sentient group (Wells 1995). In Sally R. Wigutow's story of the antique store, the owners, who were family members of the same generation, refused to talk about plans for succession for fear that talking about the next generation would disrupt their sentient ties, located in the family. Their sentience was so powerful that it trumped succession planning.

Time is an important boundary in organizations. People working the night shift are likely to have a different relationship to the organization than those who work during the day when the full complement of managerial staff is present. Sue Whittle (Chapter 5) discusses the effect of time boundaries on consulting practice and the differences between an insider's sense of time and that of an outsider. An insider is likely to have the organization-specific knowledge to know which groups work on shifts, the effect of other work demands on change initiatives, and the like. On the other hand, well-bounded interventions, with explicit beginnings, phases and endings, which are boundary markers that serve to contain the intervention, can be more difficult to realize when changing organizations from within because organizations view the insider as someone they can more easily put off, perhaps in the same way that they find their own schedules disrespected.

Green and Molenkamp write that of all the boundaries, '… the task boundary is key[.]' (3). This is where much confusion occurs between and within groups. Tasks have boundary demarcations that may change with circumstance. Andrew Day (Chapter 1) writes that change efforts often entail a decision to involve people who previously were not involved in decision-making. As CEO of Community Therapy, Victor O. Adebowale made just such a decision when he brought senior managers into discussions about organizational strategy and reached across the organization's external boundary to bring a commercial care provider into discussions about possibilities for working together (Chapter 3). The project manager in the Netherlands who oriented project participants who worked on subsystems to the progress of the project as a whole helped participants see the overall task and the relationship of sub-tasks to the over-arching goal and bounded the project meetings with a sense of order (Chapter 4). The careful attention to the whole and the creation of a good holding environment (Winnicott 1986) for the work resulted in a smoother project build. I find that using the simple term 'task' helps people focus on what they are trying to accomplish and think about whether component parts fit together or have been ignored.

A.K. Rice described the complexities of boundaries in inter-group processes (1990). A group formed of representatives of multiple departments brings together people who work in different task and sentient systems. He writes that the choice of representatives is made not only in relation to knowledge but also '… to convey the mood of the group about itself and about its representative, and its attitude …' (Rice 1990: 280). He notes that most messages will be covert rather than explicit. Thus, a group's hostility may be hidden behind its choice of a representative who is known to be contentious. The representative's snarls may be seen solely as her personality characteristic, which it is surely likely to be, rather than also as a message from and about the group. During the work, sentience changes. Representatives are not the same people they were at the start nor are the groups they left to represent in the inter-group work the same as when they left them (Rice 1990). These multiple boundaries, which invoke different interests and ways of being, make inter-group organizations, such as task forces and project teams, particularly challenging (Stevens and Whittle, Chapter 4). Rice (1990) points out that many inter-group interactions occur in circumstances where conventions and histories are well understood and therefore the potential difficulties that the complex boundary relationships pose are muted. However, as we see in Chapter 4, these factors require particular attention in projects of special importance or with a highly pressured schedule or that bring together disparate groups in novel configurations, and we articulate organization design principles that address the need for sense-making in situations of high complexity and ambiguity. The degree of intergroup complexity affects time lines: the very urgency and complexity of a project paradoxically may require a slower start-up period than a more routine project.

Authority is the 'right to do work[.]' (Green and Molenkamp 2005). They write that work becomes difficult when authority to do it is not clearly defined, taken up as authorized, or where the resources to do it are not made available, in itself a form of de-authorization. SAL Consulting (Chapter 7) felt that their invitation to work was withdrawn despite the fact that a multi-year contract was still in place. When those in power did not see value in their work, the SAL consultants felt de-authorized. Changes in who is authorized to do what are often central issues in change initiatives. Insiders may find that the language of BART helps them and their clients discuss changes in authority in a more task-focused way, one that brings organizational politics sharply into focus and available for discussion.

Internals may find themselves invited to help with more sensitive business issues as their clients get to know them: their job description hasn't changed but their clients have given them broader authority to work. Karen Izod (Chapter 8) wrote about how associates must negotiate their roles not only with client organizations but also with the host organizations for which they work.

The concept of role is closely allied with that of authority. People take up roles or find ways to resist or avoid roles. Roles are both given and taken (Krantz and Maltz 1997), that is, roles are formally designed and at the same time people take up roles in ways that are distinct from the way in which the roles are prescribed. In change initiatives, people may be expected to work in ways that may be new to them. They may shy away from parts of new jobs that make them anxious, but a supportive environment during a transition may help them learn to work in new ways and fully take up their role. There can be a lot of friction when people move into different jobs during periods of change and people who formerly worked for a laid back manager find themselves working for a Type-A personality. The role as formally defined has not changed, but the way it is taken up changes dramatically. Talking about the distinction between given and taken can help those involved understand feelings of discomfort or disorientation (I didn't have any problem doing this before).

In many chapters in this book, issues of understanding the task are central. In Sally R. Wigutow's Chapter 6, she asks whether the antique store owners' task is to run the business or sustain the family. Pauline Holland writes that the primary task in her organization shifted as external circumstances changed and that there was rarely one primary task. In Victor O. Adebowale's case study (Chapter 3), the primary task expanded and required that senior managers learn to negotiate service provider contracts and understand costs. The speech therapist/project manager in Chapter 4 saw that his client's task was too daunting and realized that he had to reframe it into something more doable to make the ultimate goal achievable. Where emotions overwhelm, tasks feel impossible (Hirschhorn 1988).

The task is the aim toward which work is directed or the purpose of the work, which may be stated explicitly and/or enacted tacitly. Sub-units within an organization may define their primary task explicitly as some component of the organization's larger task while working furiously to defend themselves against corporate 'interference' in their work. A trading unit in a bank may make progressively riskier trades while rebuffing inquiries from the bank's risk management group. To say that reconciling component tasks with other tasks and linking them to the organization's overall task is often problematic is an understatement. It is often the heart of organizational problems requiring a change effort, as it was in Andrew Day's case (Chapter 1). Where work is organized as projects and people find themselves working in new and different ways, visualizing work flows can help people see the whole (Stevens and Whittle, Chapter 4). In a similar vein, governance structures and processes can facilitate the management of the project as a whole.

The BART terminology and the rich concepts it embraces provide an accessible way for insiders to recognize and talk about issues that are pervasive in organizational change efforts: how definitions of task, who has what role and authority, and how boundaries might have to shift in order to achieve the desired change. BART can also help people see the organization's relationship to its environment, the system within which it exists. It helps them understand how dependent they are on transactions across their organizational boundary: many projects cannot be accomplished without services and supplies from other organizations. The organization requires employees with requisite skills, many of whom will be trained by external educational providers. The organization is affected by legislation and may want to ally itself with others in its industry in trade associations to influence legislators.

Remembering that Organizations are Open Systems

In the 1940s and 1950s, systems thinking was established as a major scientific movement (Capra 1996). Systems concepts came to the notice of the Tavistock Institute in 1950 and soon were integrated into the Institute's work on the nature of organizations (Fraher 2004). Whereas classical organization theory saw organizations as closed systems, independent of the environment, open systems theory requires study of the organization in its environment (Miller 1993). This book has any number of examples showing the importance of understanding the external environments of organizations. Decisions by donors to withdraw funding required Victor O. Adebowale's Community Therapy (Chapter 3) to make major changes to survive. Changes in the external environment also forced changes in the social services organization where Pauline Holland instituted an internal consulting service (Chapter 2). Helping organizations face environmental shifts requires that people learn to work in different and perhaps uncomfortable ways. SAL Consulting (Chapter 7) uses their Organizational Relational Assessment Tool to scan the environment to assess the clients' readiness or non-readiness to work with SAL.

Boundary is a key concept in systems thinking (Miller 1993). Organizations interact with their environment across boundaries. Pauline Holland's organization became more externally oriented as it sought funds in an increasingly competitive environment. That orientation was reflected in the change in its practices from a supervision model to one where business meetings predominated (Chapter 2). Many projects rely on external suppliers and consultants. If an organization maintains only limited contacts with suppliers and does not seek to understand their concerns and offerings and/ or communicate well about its own needs and concerns, it may find that it cannot deliver successful projects: it has not managed its relationship with the external environment in an effective manner. External forces can sink projects despite the best internal preparations, as we saw in Chapter 4 when the UK national government '… announced massive funding reductions to [children's] services[.]' (Stevens and Whittle: 81, in this book). Consultants and change agents may need to help clients strengthen boundaries, to prevent dissipation from demand and disturbances outside, or loosen a boundary (such as what business we are in or who can make decisions) to allow the client organization to relate to their environment more effectively. That environment might comprise other groups within the same organization, suppliers, or some other entity.

Skilled consultants draw attention to the myths and realities of 'the environment' and may need to challenge their client's and their own perceptions of task, organization, role and authority boundaries.

Implications for Consultancy Practice

Our goal in writing this book was to hear from organizational change practitioners about their experiences and the techniques and strategies they have used to work as insiders. We have seen the rich variety of ways in which they practice and the many different settings for their work. Although we did not set out to build consulting theory, I believe that we have started down that road.

We have seen how much insiders have to manage in their relationships with the organizations that they work in or with. Many are slotted into an organizational hierarchy and have relationships with bosses, subordinates and colleagues to think about. Others, even though contractually external, become attached to or feel part of the organizations that are their clients and/ or find that their clients treat them like insiders. Still others relate to client organizations through host organizations that may colour their relationship with the client organization. When insiders are alert to how organizational culture influences them and how the pushes and pulls of projective processes between them and organization members affect them and their work, they have the possibility to consult more effectively. If I understand how the emotional experience that is part of group life affects organization members and me, I have a broader repertoire of theory to use in addressing the issues that arise during organizational change.

Theory helps consultants live with and tolerate their own anxiety about not knowing so that they can help their clients do the same. (Andrew Day in Chapter 1, Pauline Holland in Chapter 2, and I in Chapter 4 describe being anxious about our ability to consult effectively.) Theory reminds us where to look and how to engage with the data we find and experiences we have before applying a 'solution' that came from work with a seemingly similar client we had two years ago. It helps us recognize how our own experiences colour the meaning we ascribe to what we observe in organizations. (Senge et al.'s Ladder of Inference offers a useful model of how we build beliefs (1994).) Theory is essential for sorting out what is going on and determining how to intervene to bring about change. The rich theory from the worlds of psychoanalysis, group relations and systems thinking helps insiders appreciate the dynamics of organizational change and enables them to work with their clients in a mind-ful (Whittle and Izod 2009) way as they seek to improve their organizations.

As organizations and their members are stressed by their environments and have expectations that they will quickly adapt to change, I think they will welcome consultants who can help them understand the welter of events, who remember that it is human beings that do the work of organizations, and who can help them navigate the waters in a way that makes use of the sorts of theories I have elucidated here.

References

Alderfer, C. 1987. An intergroup perspective on group dynamics, in *Handbook of Organizational Behavior*, edited by J.W. Lorsch. Englewood Cliffs, NJ: Prentice-Hall, 190–222.

Armstrong, D. 2005. *Organization in the Mind: Psychoanalysis, Group Relations and Organizational Consultancy*. London: Karnac Books Ltd.

Bion, W.R. 1961. *Experiences in Groups and Other Papers*. London: Tavistock Publications Limited.

Capra, F. 1996. *The Web of Life*. New York, London, Toronto, Sydney and Auckland: Anchor Books Doubleday.

Durkheim, E. (Lukes, S., ed., Halls, W.D., trans.) 1982. *The Rules of the Sociological Method*. New York: Free Press.

Fraher, A.L. 2004. Systems psychodynamics: The formative years (1895–1967). *Organizational & Social Dynamics*, 4(2), 191–211.

Frosh, S. 2003. *Key Concepts in Psychoanalysis*. New York: New York University Press.

Green, Z.G. and Molenkamp, R.J. 2005. *The BART System of Group and Organizational Analysis: Boundary, Authority, Role and Task* [Online]. Available at: http://www.it.uu.se/edu/course/homepage/projektDV/ht09/BART_Green _Molenkamp.pdf [accessed: May 26, 2012].

Hayden, C. and Molenkamp, R.J. 2002. *Tavistock Primer* II. Jupiter, FL: The A.K. Rice Institute for the Study of Social Systems.

Heifetz, R.A. 1994. *Leadership Without Easy Answers*. Boston, MA: Harvard University Press.

Hirschhorn, L. 1988. *The Workplace Within: Psychodynamics of Organizational Life*. Cambridge, MA: The MIT Press.

Krantz, J. and Maltz, M. 1997. A framework for consulting to organizational role. *Consulting Psychology Journal, Practice and Research*, 49(2), 137–51.

Marris, P. 1974. *Loss and Change*. New York: Pantheon Books.

Miller, E. 1993. *From Dependency to Autonomy: Studies in Organization and Change*. London: Free Association Books.

Miller, E.J. and Rice, A.K. 1990. Task and sentient systems and their boundary controls, in *The Social Engagement of Social Science: A Tavistock Anthology, Volume 1: The Socio-Psychological Perspective*, edited by E. Trist and H. Murray. Philadelphia, PA: The University of Pennsylvania Press, 259–71.

Rice, A.K. 1990. Individual, group and inter-group processes, in *The Social Engagement of Social Science: A Tavistock Anthology, Volume 1: The Socio-Psychological Perspective*, edited by E. Trist and H. Murray. Philadelphia, PA: The University of Pennsylvania Press, 272–84.

Schein, E. 1988. *Process Consultation, Volume I: Its Role in Organizational Development*. Reading, MA; Menlo Park, CA; New York; Don Mills, Ontario; Wokingham, England; Amsterdam; Bonn; Sydney; Singapore; Tokyo; Madrid; San Juan: Addison-Wesley Publishing Company.

Senge, P.M., Kleiner, A., Roberts, C., Ross, R.B. and Smith, B.J. 2004. *The Fifth Discipline Fieldbook: Strategies and Tools for Building a Learning Organization*. New York, London, Toronto, Sydney, Auckland: Doubleday.

Singer, D.L. and Shapiro, E.R. 1989. *Discovering the Links Between Early Family Roles and Current Organizational Roles: A Loved and Feared Task*. Paper to the 1989 Spring Symposium of the Center for the Study of Groups and Social Systems (the Boston Center of the A.K. Rice Institute), Boston, April 1, 1989.

Wells, L., Jr. 1995. The group as a whole: A systematic socioanalytic perspective on interpersonal and group relations, in *Groups in Context: A New Perspective on Group Dynamics*, edited by J. Gillette and M. McCollom. Lanham, New York, and London: University Press of America Inc., 49–85.

Whittle, S. 2009. The challenge of a mind-ful approach to organizational consulting, in *Mind-ful Consulting*, edited by S. Whittle and K. Izod, London: Karnac, xxi–xxxiii.

Winnicott, D.W. (compiled and edited by C. Winnicott, R. Shepherd, and M. Davis) 1986. *Home is Where We Start From: Essays by a Psychoanalyst.* New York and London: W.W. Norton & Company.

Index

For Product Safety Concerns and Information please contact our EU representative GPSR@taylorandfrancis.com Taylor & Francis Verlag GmbH, Kaufingerstraße 24, 80331 München, Germany

Printed and bound by CPI Group (UK) Ltd, Croydon, CR0 4YY

01/05/2025

01858426-0011